PHILADELPHIA
COCKTAILS

AN ELEGANT COLLECTION OF
OVER 100 RECIPES INSPIRED BY
THE CITY OF BROTHERLY LOVE

TRAVIS MITCHELL

PHILADELPHIA COCKTAILS

Copyright © 2025 by Cider Mill Press Book Publishers LLC.

This is an officially licensed book by Cider Mill Press Book Publishers LLC.

All rights reserved under the Pan-American and International Copyright Conventions.

No part of this book may be reproduced in whole or in part, scanned, photocopied, recorded, distributed in any printed or electronic form, or reproduced in any manner whatsoever, or by any information storage and retrieval system now known or hereafter invented, without express written permission of the publisher, except in the case of brief quotations embodied in critical articles and reviews.

The scanning, uploading, and distribution of this book via the internet or via any other means without permission of the publisher is illegal and punishable by law. Please support authors' rights, and do not participate in or encourage piracy of copyrighted materials.

ISBN-13: 978-1-40034-064-4
ISBN-10: 1-40034-064-0

This book may be ordered by mail from the publisher. Please include $5.99 for postage and handling. Please support your local bookseller first!

Books published by Cider Mill Press Book Publishers are available at special discounts for bulk purchases in the United States by corporations, institutions, and other organizations. For more information, please contact the publisher.

Cider Mill Press Book Publishers
"Where good books are ready for press"
501 Nelson Place
Nashville, Tennessee 37214
cidermillpress.com

Typography: Headline Gothic ATF, Copperplate, Sackers, Warnock

Photography credits on page 248

Printed in India

25 26 27 28 29 REP 5 4 3 2 1

First Edition

CONTENTS

INTRODUCTION · 5

CENTER CITY / RITTENHOUSE SQUARE /
LOGAN SQUARE · 19

OLD CITY / SOCIETY HILL /
PENN'S LANDING · 105

SOUTH STREET / QUEEN VILLAGE /
SOUTH PHILLY · 147

NORTH PHILLY / SPRING GARDEN /
NORTHERN LIBERTIES / FISHTOWN /
SUBURBS · 176

INDEX · 249

INTRODUCTION

Philadelphia is a proud and passionate city. From its central role in American history to its beloved sports teams and musicians, the city's cultural influence has been undeniable from its earliest days. It's an energy you feel walking past Independence Hall, where the Declaration of Independence was signed in the summer of 1776 and where the Constitution was signed in 1787. It's an energy you feel on Sunday afternoons each fall, when devoted football fans gather in hopes of a championship season. And these days, it's an energy you feel when exploring the city's vibrant bars and restaurants, fueled by some of the country's most talented bartenders.

For all the city's historical significance, Philadelphia's contributions to America's food and drink scene find themselves draped in the shadow of larger cities like New York or Los Angeles. Even smaller locales, like Washington, DC, and New Orleans, have attracted national acclaim that too often eludes Philadelphia. When people do praise Philadelphia's culinary identity, it's common to overhear the greatest hits playlist of cheesesteaks, soft pretzels, and beer. But there is so much more to appreciate, taste, and drink.

In true Rocky Balboa form, Philly's hospitality community is eager to embrace and overcome the underdog role. It's a city that's hungry—or rather, thirsty—for its time in the spotlight.

HOW TO STOCK YOUR PHILADELPHIA HOME BAR

Philadelphia and the surrounding areas are home to a bounty of spirits and bartending products. Many of them are recommended throughout this book. A setup could include items such as:

BLUECOAT AMERICAN DRY GIN: produced by Philadelphia Distilling

VIEUX CARRÉ ABSINTHE SUPÉRIEURE: produced by Philadelphia Distilling

SELECT FOUR GRAIN AMERICAN WHISKEY: produced by Manatawny Still Works

GIN FINISHED IN OAK BARRELS: produced by Manatawny Still Works

BEE STING CIDER: produced by Hale & True Cider Co.

VERMOUTHS: produced by Fell to Earth

STATESIDE URBANCRAFT VODKA: produced by Federal Distilling

Because Philadelphia is a "control state," the majority of liquor sales are through official state stores (Fine Wine & Good Spirits). Distilleries are also permitted to sell their products to tasting room and bottle shop visitors.

BASIC PREPARATIONS & TECHNIQUES

BASIC STIRRING: Stirring is used to mix cocktails without the additional aeration you'd get from a shake. Stirring is important both for dilution and for temperature control. A good stir should happen over ice for about ten seconds, until the drink feels chilled.

BASIC SHAKING: Shaking a cocktail not only blends the ingredients together, it also achieves dilution and aeration. It also helps to chill a drink to its ideal temperature. Most recipes with fresh juices, citrus, or egg whites will call for shaking before serving. Cocktail mixing tins come in two parts, which are joined together for shaking. Be sure to hold on tight and shake away from your body. Shake drinks vigorously over ice for ten to fifteen seconds for best results.

DRY SHAKE: Some cocktail recipes use a dry shake. This technique is simply shaking a cocktail without ice to optimize aeration. It creates a frothy texture when working with ingredients like egg whites. A wet shake, then, is a shake with ice.

STRAIN: Straining a drink with a Hawthorne strainer after shaking or stirring keeps unwanted ingredients—think ice cubes, mint leaves, and citrus seeds—from entering your cocktail. Straining is not always required. Some drinks, like the Smash, are best served "dirty," with bits of fruit and shaken ice melding together. The decision is really a matter of considering the overall ingredients used and how you would like the final drink to look and taste.

DOUBLE STRAIN: Also known as a fine strain, double-straining is a method used to remove fine particles, such as ice chips or fruit pulp, from the cocktail. The most common method of double-straining is to use one hand to pour the contents of the cocktail tin through a Hawthorne strainer while holding a fine-mesh strainer in the other hand. Be sure the drink liquid passes through both strainers. You can also achieve a fine strain by using a mesh strainer on its own.

Juicing Citrus: Any bartender will tell you that fresh citrus is superior to store-bought options. For recipes that call for lemon or lime juice, use whole fruit whenever possible. A handheld citrus squeezer is an affordable bartending tool that will easily up the quality of your finished cocktails. As a general rule, a single lemon or lime yields about one ounce of fresh juice.

Salting a Rim: A salt rim adds flavor and texture to a cocktail and can be salty, savory, sweet, or spicy, depending on the ingredients used. To begin, wet the outer edge of the glass using a wedge of lemon, lime, or other citrus. This provides better adhesion than water, which is not sticky enough to hold salt. Next, place your prepared rim garnish on a plate and roll your glass back and forth until the rim is coated. As obvious as it sounds, be sure to rim your glass while it is still empty.

Simple Syrup: Simple syrup is the workhouse sweetener of cocktails. Simple syrup uses a ratio of one part white sugar to one part water, and it can be made easily on the stovetop by gently heating the sugar and water together, stirring, until the sugar is dissolved. To make rich simple syrup, which has a more viscous texture, double the ratio, using two parts of white sugar to one part water. And to make demerara syrup, swap out the white sugar with demerara sugar, a dark cane sugar with flavors of caramel and molasses, in the simple syrup recipe. Again, to make rich demerara syrup, double the amount of sugar respective to the amount of water. For all syrups, store them in the refrigerator and use them within one to two weeks.

Honey Syrup: In a small saucepan, combine 1 cup almost-boiling water with 1 cup honey and stir until the honey is dissolved. Then allow the syrup to cool.

Saline Solution: Combine water and salt at a ratio of 4:1, i.e., 80 grams (80 ml) water with 20 grams salt (table salt, kosher, sea salt—your choice) and stir until the salt is dissolved. For a weaker saline solution, use a ratio of 4.5:1 or 5:1. Keep the solution in a dropper bottle for ease of use.

THE HISTORY OF COCKTAILS IN PHILADELPHIA

The founding fathers appreciated a good drink as much as anyone. During colonial times, taverns were a spot to partake in a few rounds between friends as well as get the inside scoop on politics and gossip.

Philadelphia's most recognized cocktail is likely the Fish House Punch, popularized by George Washington. A recipe held by his Mount Vernon residence cites a recipe from the State in Schuylkill (often referred to as the Schuylkill Fishing Company), a Pennsylvania social club founded in 1732. The potent punch calls for 2 quarts of Jamaican rum, 1 quart of cognac, ¾ pound of "loaf sugar," 2 quarts of water, 1 quart of lemon or lime juice, and a wineglass measure of peach brandy.

The Pennsylvania Statehouse (Independence Hall) in 1778

Following the passing of the Twenty-First Amendment and the repeal of Prohibition, Philadelphia saw the birth of one of the world's most recognized rye whiskeys. In 1934, the Continental Distilling Company of Philadelphia introduced Rittenhouse Square Straight Rye Whisky, naming it for the city's historic Rittenhouse Square. Those first bottles were two-year-old 100-proof rye whiskeys. In 1948, the company transitioned to selling a four-year bottled-in-bond product and simplified the name to Rittenhouse Rye. The brand was purchased by Kentucky's Heaven Hill Distillery in 1993, and it continues to be a go-to option behind both home and professional bars.

CITY TAVERN

Operating from 1774 to around 1800, Philadelphia's City Tavern was a favorite spot for food, drink, and refuge among politicians and those traveling through on business. Also known as the Merchant's Coffee House, the building was located at the intersection of 2nd and Walnut streets. It's no longer a bar, but its story lives on as part of Independence National Historic Park.

It was at City Tavern that the Pennsylvania State Society of the Cincinnati was founded on October 4, 1783. The Pennsylvania chapter of the fraternal organization was the ninth of thirteen chapters, each made up of Continental army officers with the intent to "perpetuate the memory of the War for Independence." The organization elected General George Washington as its president general at a meeting in September of the same year. He would serve in that position until his death in 1799.

As tastes changed, City Tavern's clientele migrated and dispersed to more modern options. A fire badly damaged the building in 1834, and the original structure lasted a couple more decades before being torn down in 1854. A reconstruction opened in 1976 to commemorate the United States bicentennial. It operated as a historically accurate restaurant for a time, closing in 2020 due to the pandemic. Today, it remains on display as a historic site where visitors can meander around the exterior or through the small garden.

A 1908 depiction of Philadelphia's famous eighteenth-century City Tavern in Old City

THE CLOVER CLUB

The Clover Club was born the evening of Thursday, December 29, 1881, when thirteen gentlemen gathered at the Girard House to share a meal and organize a dining club. Its rich and colorful history was documented in Mary R. Deacon's 1897 publishing of *The Clover Club of Philadelphia*. Deacon was the daughter of Charles Deacon, who served as club secretary between February 1882 and May 1896.

Deacon wrote that the club was founded as a space for "social enjoyments, the cultivation of literary tastes, and the encouragement of hospitable intercourse" and that the name came from an appreciation for the use of clover across science, nature, and art. "The word pronounced has a fullness and a sweetness," she said.

The Clover Club banquet room at the Bellevue-Stratford Hotel, 1905

In April 1882, the Clover Club held dinner at The Hotel Bellevue for the first time. Dinner rituals included the passing around of the "loving cup," a silver tankard filled with a potent and strong cocktail that members described as having "penetrating properties and enervating powers" for those who dared indulge with multiple sips.

As of 1897, club membership ranged from newspaper editors to lawyers and medical professionals. "Humor, wit, ability are confined to no calling in the United States," Deacon wrote. The club gained a reputation for its spirited, humorous, and joyful dinners. Drinking was no doubt a part of the experience, but so was moderation. In Deacon's words, "The Clover Club never gets intoxicated—never."

The club's legacy lives on in the cocktail of the same name. The gin, lemon, and raspberry sour traces its story back to the Bellevue and can be found on bar menus around Philadelphia to this day.

Members-only social clubs endure as part of modern Philadelphia nightlife. Names like Palizzi Social Club, Pen & Pencil Club, and the Acorn Club carry on the tradition of food, drink, and fellowship, often into the early hours of the morning.

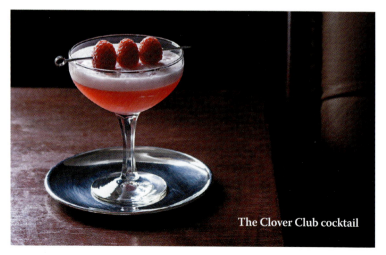

The Clover Club cocktail

COCKTAILS IN MODERN-DAY PHILADELPHIA

The City of Brotherly Love will always have its blue-collar DNA. Neighborhood pubs slinging cold beers and Citywides aren't about to vanish. But today, the city is riding a craft cocktail swell that's impossible to ignore.

The momentum started with spots like Franklin Mortgage and Investment Company, which opened its doors in 2009 and brought speakeasy vibes to Rittenhouse Square. That original address (the bar reopened nearby after the pandemic) was notable as the first project of Proprietors LLC, a bar consultancy firm run by cocktail powerhouses David Kaplan and Alex Day of Death & Co fame. A year later, in 2010, prolific local restaurateur Stephen Starr revealed the dark and moody Ranstead Room. The bar debuted with a menu crafted by the late Sasha Petraske, the renowned New York City bartender and Milk & Honey founder who sparked the modern cocktail revival. These events set the tone for what the city's scene could become. Now, these bars and others like them are evolving and thriving under a new generation of ambition and talent.

When it comes to cocktails, Philadelphia bartenders are a creative and resourceful bunch. They are keen to experiment with just about any flavor or techniques. Recipes in this book feature ingredients like beet-and-carrot-infused gin, white chocolate–washed rum, and masala chai syrup. A reverence for classics is apparent in remixes like a kombu broth–accented margarita and a Manhattan that uses both rye whiskey and mezcal. Seasonality comes into play, with many bar programs working hand-in-hand with their kitchen counterparts to shake and stir drinks that enhance the guest experience from start to finish. The bar community also takes care to use local products when possible, taking advantage of the robust brewing and distilling options.

Today, outstanding cocktails can be found across the city, whether it's at an upscale hotel lobby in City Center, an acclaimed restaurant in Rittenhouse Square, or a buzzy lounge in Fishtown.

CENTER CITY / RITTENHOUSE SQUARE / LOGAN SQUARE

Signed, Sealed, Delivered	Done and Dusted
Lawless Doings	Sip Your Sins
Charmed, I'm Sure	Awaji-Musubi
Waiting for the Moon to Rise	The Butcher
The Sacred Cow	Kimono Racer
Best Served Cold 2.0	Agave Vesper
Fish House Punch	Sacrifice to the Gods
Mezcal Margarita	Neck Brace
Paloma	Bombay Moon
Siam Spritz	Raspberry Lychee Bellini
Seadog	Ginger Margarita
10th Street Stretch	Astronaut
Italian Market Espresso Martini	Frozen Blood Orange Margarita
Deranged Lumberjack Old Fashioned	Felipe Collins
Free Bird (NA)	BP Manhattan
Haymaker	Spritz Royale
French Breakfast	Old Fashioned
Margarita Vert	Investment Manhattan
Persian Paloma	Pimm's Deluxe
	Piña Colada

The neighborhoods of City Center, Rittenhouse Square, and Logan Square can be considered Philadelphia's downtown. Here, you'll find luxury hotels, skyscrapers, and some of the city's trailblazing cocktail bars, including Ranstead Room and The Franklin Mortgage. But the biggest landmark of all is the nineteenth-century masterpiece, Philadelphia City Hall, standing proud at the heart of the city and dominated by the thirty-seven-foot-tall statue of William Penn, who founded the City of Brotherly Love over three centuries ago. The SkyHigh Lounge, sixty floors above street level, features what may be Philly's best views. City Center also includes South 13th Street, a densely packed stretch of can't-miss bars and restaurants for all budgets.

SIGNED, SEALED, DELIVERED

LOCH BAR
301 SOUTH BROAD STREET

Loch Bar is known for its seafood plates and luxury raw bar options more fitting of an oceanside dining room than a downtown restaurant. Andrew Nichols, head of mixology for parent company Atlas Restaurant Group, creates cocktails that fit that same vibe—with standbys like an Orange Crush alongside more complex recipes like this one, which finds friendship in flavors of Cognac and banana. And, like all the bar's specialty cocktails, it takes its name from popular music.

GLASSWARE: Nick & Nora glass
GARNISH: Grated nutmeg

- 1½ oz. Pierre Ferrand 1840 Cognac
- ½ oz. Tempus Fugit Crème de Banane
- ¼ oz. Planteray Xaymaca Special Dry Jamaican Rum
- ½ oz. fresh lemon juice
- ¼ oz. Barbadillo Oloroso Sherry
- Dash Scrappy's Chocolate Bitters

1. Chill a Nick & Nora glass. Combine all of the ingredients in a shaking tin, then add ice and shake.

2. Double-strain the cocktail into the chilled Nick & Nora.

3. Gently grate nutmeg over the surface of the drink.

NICO DIAZ, RANSTEAD ROOM

Nico Diaz is the head bartender at Ranstead Room.

What do you enjoy most about bartending?

Having the opportunity to make someone's night is pretty special to me. The guest experience is a critical component to it all—it's how we turn casual visitors into regulars. Also, there's a certain rhythm to bartending in a flow state that I've always loved.

What tips and tricks do you have for home bartenders? Is there a secret to making a great cocktail?

I'd advise using fresh, quality ingredients and to place an emphasis on balance, mouthfeel, and temperature.

What do you enjoy most about the Philadelphia cocktail community?

Philly's a drinking city. It's relatively easy to find a well-made cocktail. The scene here is vibrant and growing and beginning to step firmly into its sophistication.

LAWLESS DOINGS

RANSTEAD ROOM
2013 RANSTEAD STREET

Ranstead Room head bartender Nico Diaz originally created this drink in 2021 while working for Bluecoat Gin. It has evolved into a guest favorite at Ranstead Room and has been featured on special menus across the U.S., including at the Violet Hour in Chicago, Service Bar in Washington, the Fox Bar in Nashville, and Natasha's Gin Room in St. Louis. Mango-infused gin and a healthy dose of fresh mint make this tiki-inspired Highball a well-balanced refresher.

GLASSWARE: Collins glass
GARNISH: Mint bouquet, skull pick, dehydrated lime wheel

- 2 oz. Mango-Infused Gin (see recipe)
- ¾ oz. fresh lime juice
- ¾ oz. Demerara Simple Syrup (see recipe on page 11)
- 1 handful mint
- 2 dashes Amaro Sfumato Rabarbaro
- Splash soda water, to top

1. Freeze a collins glass. Combine all of the ingredients, except for the soda water, in a cocktail shaker with a single chip or small cube of ice.
2. Whip-shake until the ice cube is completely melted.
3. Pour the cocktail into the frozen collins glass, then fill the glass with pebbled ice.
4. Top with soda water and garnish with a mint bouquet, skull pick, and dehydrated lime wheel

MANGO-INFUSED GIN: Combine 225 grams dried natural mango and 1 liter London dry gin. Cover and let the infusion sit at ambient temperature for 72 hours. Strain through a cheesecloth.

CHARMED, I'M SURE

RANSTEAD ROOM
2013 RANSTEAD STREET

This cocktail is both complex in flavor and austere in its simplicity. The final product is all about balance and temperature, says Ranstead Room lead bartender Nico Diaz. The recipe calls for Paranubes Oaxaca Rum, which can be tricky to source. To affect Paranubes's grassy notes, Diaz recommends substituting a rhum agricole.

GLASSWARE: Nick & Nora glass

- Honey, for the glass
- Black sea salt, for the glass
- 1¼ oz. mezcal
- 1 oz. Amaro Montenegro
- ½ oz. Paranubes Blanco Rum
- ¼ oz. Chareau
- 4 dashes APP Bitters (see recipe)

1. Freeze a Nick & Nora glass, brush honey in a stripe on the side of the glass, then dip the stripe in black sea salt.
2. Combine the remaining ingredients in a mixing glass with ice.
3. Stir well until diluted and chilled, 10 to 15 seconds.
4. Strain the cocktail into the frozen Nick & Nora.
5. Serve up.

APP BITTERS: In a small jar or dropper bottle, combine equal parts Angostura bitters, Peychaud's bitters, and Dale DeGroff's Pimento Aromatic Bitters.

WEI-WEI WEINTRAUB, FRANKLIN MORTGAGE AND INVESTMENT COMPANY

Wei-Wei Weintraub is a bartender at Franklin Mortgage and Investment Company.

How did you get started in bartending?

In early 2018, I started working as a server and then manager at the original location of The Franklin Mortgage and Investment Company at 18th & Sansom Street. I had been working in the industry since the age of fifteen, but never in cocktail bars. My interest in spirits grew quickly, and the bartenders there gave me the opportunity to start working on menus and taught me how to bartend. I'm very grateful to the past head bartenders who took me in.

What do you enjoy most about bartending?

The creative aspect is what I love most. I have a degree in painting, and there are a lot of similarities in constructing drinks and paintings. When guests are genuinely interested in the process and also in learning about spirits, those conversations are what makes bartending most enjoyable.

What tips and tricks do you have for home bartenders? Is there a secret to making a great cocktail?

I think the best tip I can give is, don't be too attached to an idea or an outcome of a cocktail during the development stages. Trusting the process and pivoting to different ideas are all part of that. I also really love collaborating with people, because it opens up other pathways to new directions you may not have thought of. Stay open and have fun. Obviously balance, taste, and smell (all senses) are important with the final result of a cocktail, but staying open can lead to great ideas. Your experiences shape your cocktails also, so explore the world and always try new things.

What do you enjoy most about the Philadelphia cocktail community?

We are that—a community. Philly's cocktail scene has always been small but everyone in this community is extremely supportive of one another.

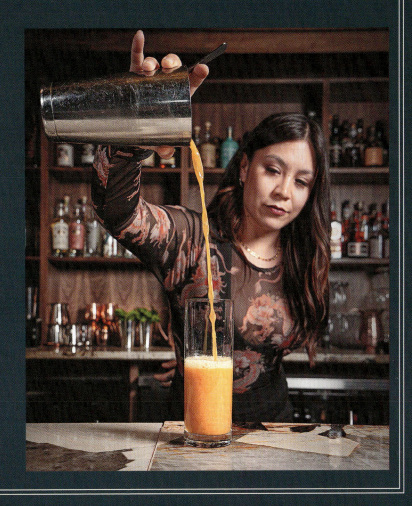

WAITING FOR THE MOON TO RISE

THE FRANKLIN MORTGAGE & INVESTMENT COMPANY
1715 RITTENHOUSE SQUARE

For this fall-inspired cocktail, Bartender Wei-wei Weintraub wanted to play with spirits and flavors not typically found in tropical drinks. Instead of being rum-forward and fruity, it showcases both blended and peated Scotch whisky together with an acidic fresh Granny Smith apple cordial. Freshly grated nutmeg and an aromatic smoked cinnamon stick further lift the senses.

GLASSWARE: Collins glass
GARNISH: Pineapple frond, Granny Smith apple slice, grated nutmeg, smoked cinnamon stick

- 1¼ oz. Monkey Shoulder
- ½ oz. Laphroaig 10
- ¼ oz. Giffard Caribbean Pineapple Liqueur
- ½ oz. fresh lemon juice
- ¾ oz. Granny Smith Apple Cordial (see recipe)
- Splash prosecco, to top

1. Combine all of the ingredients, except for the prosecco, in a cocktail shaker with ice and shake until chilled and diluted, about 10 seconds.
2. Strain the cocktail into a collins glass and fill with crushed ice. Top with prosecco.
3. Garnish with a pineapple frond, Granny Smith apple slice, grated nutmeg, and a smoked cinnamon stick.

Granny Smith Apple Cordial: In a pot over medium-low heat, combine ½ cup fresh Granny Smith apple juice and 1 cup white sugar and heat lightly, stirring until the sugar is dissolved. Remove from heat and allow the mixture to cool. Using a kitchen scale, add 0.02% malic acid by weight of the finished cordial.

THE SACRED COW

THE FRANKLIN MORTGAGE & INVESTMENT COMPANY
1715 RITTENHOUSE SQUARE

This recipe combines cool, spicy chai tea with rum and coconut for an exuberant, refreshing overall effect—homemade foam and all.

GLASSWARE: Rocks glass
GARNISH: Almond dust

- 1½ oz. Cacao Nibs–Infused Rum (see recipe)
- ½ oz. Kalani Coconut Liqueur
- ½ oz. orgeat
- ¼ oz. ginger syrup
- ½ oz. fresh lemon Juice
- Masala chai tea, to top
- Coconut Foam (see recipe), to top

1. Combine all of the ingredients, except for the Coconut Foam and masala chai tea, in a container and measure the liquid volume.
2. Add an equal volume of masala chai tea to the container and let the mixture sit for a few hours to clarify.
3. Strain using a Chemex or similar filter to clarify.
4. Pour the cocktail over a large ice cube into a rocks glass, top with the Coconut Foam, and then garnish with a light layer of almond dust.

COCONUT FOAM: In a glass container, combine 200 grams coconut milk, 100 grams coconut water, 24 ml Simple Syrup (see recipe on page 11), 5 grams yogurt, and ¼ lemon peel and mix well. Let the mixture sit for 30 minutes to 1 hour in the refrigerator. Fine-strain and add the mixture into the iSi whipped cream canister and add two N_2O charges. Let it sit for 20 minutes before using.

CACAO NIBS–INFUSED RUM: In a large glass container, combine 1 liter El Dorado 5 Year Old Rum and 100 grams cacao nibs and let it infuse for 24 hours at room temperature. Strain.

BEST SERVED COLD 2.0

THE FRANKLIN MORTGAGE & INVESTMENT COMPANY
1715 RITTENHOUSE SQUARE

Starting with gin and white vermouth like a Martini, this luxury concoction keeps going, featuring an Icelandic aquavit and more than one rather unique ingredient: smoked salmon–infused gin, and a creative "caviar."

GLASSWARE: Collins glass
GARNISH: Dill sprig, Red Pickled Onion Caviar (see recipe)

- 2 oz. Lox-Infused Gin (see recipe)
- ¾ oz. Marolo Ulrich Vermouth Bianco
- ¼ oz. Brennivín
- 1 teaspoon Dill Tincture (see recipe)

1. Combine all of the ingredients in a mixing glass with ice.
2. Stir until chilled, about 15 seconds.
3. Strain the cocktail into a collins glass over a large rock.
4. Garnish with a dill sprig and accompany with a spoon of onion caviar.

Lox-Infused Gin: In a large liquid storage container or bottle, combine 30 grams smoked salmon with 1 (750 ml) bottle of Beefeater Gin. Allow the mixture to infuse in the refrigerator for 24 hours. Strain well, using a Chemex or fine-mesh strainer.

Dill Tincture: In a liquid storage container, combine 1 (750 ml) bottle of 100-proof vodka and 50 grams dill. Allow the mixture to infuse for 1 week. Strain using a Chemex or fine-mesh strainer.

RED PICKLED ONION CAVIAR: In a pot over medium-low heat, combine 1 cup red vinegar, ½ cup water, 1 teaspoon salt, ½ cup sugar, 5 whole cloves, 5 bay leaves, ½ teaspoon black peppercorns, and ½ teaspoon pink peppercorns. Bring the mixture to a simmer. Pour the finished product into a jar with 1 red onion, sliced. Cover and refrigerate overnight. Chill 1 cup canola oil in the refrigerator. The next day, strain the pickling juice into a small pot over medium-high heat. Whisk in 1 teaspoon agar agar and bring the liquid to a boil. Remove the mixture from heat and set it aside for 5 minutes. Transfer the warm liquid to a squeeze bottle and drizzle it into the chilled canola oil. This will create the spheres. Strain and rinse the spheres in cold water, then store them in the leftover pickle juice. Refrigerate and store for up to 3 days.

FISH HOUSE PUNCH

VERNICK FISH
ONE NORTH 19TH STREET

The Fish House punch dates back to 1732 and the Schuylkill Fishing Company. Vernick Fish and bartender Jon Bamonte give a modern treatment to the classic Philadelphia beverage by substituting the standard peach brandy for a house recipe that steeps peach tea into classic brandy with the addition of cane sugar and St-Germain. The result is a fresher and more fragrant peach flavor that also adds a layer of tannins for a strong and refreshing finish.

GLASSWARE: Footed punch glass
GARNISH: Lemon wedge

- 1 oz. Pierre Ferrand 1840 Original Formula Cognac
- 1 oz. Myers's Rum Original Dark
- ¾ oz. fresh lemon juice
- ½ oz. Planteray O.F.T.D. Overproof Rum
- ½ oz. Peach Brandy (see recipe)

1. Combine all of the ingredients in a cocktail shaker with ice.
2. Shake well until chilled and combined, about 15 seconds
3. Strain the cocktail into a footed punch glass and garnish with a lemon wedge.

PEACH BRANDY: In a large jar or kitchen storage container, combine 1 (750 ml) bottle of Spanish brandy, 1 oz. rishi peach tea, 1 cup Simple Syrup (see recipe on page 11), and 1 cup elderflower liqueur and mix well.

MEZCAL MARGARITA

CONDESA AND EL TECHO
1830 LUDLOW STREET

Bartender Stephen Pressman's take on the margarita puts mezcal in the forefront. All of the margaritas at Condesa & El Techo are served on draft and made with fresh lime juice and a touch of dark amber agave nectar. A splash of Combier orange liqueur rounds out the recipe in place of sugary additives like traditional triple sec or sweet and sour mix.

GLASSWARE: Margarita glass
GARNISH: Lime wedge

- Maldon Sea Salt Flakes and a lime wedge, for the rim
- Thin slice of cucumber
- 2 oz. Banhez Ensamble
- ¾ oz. fresh lime juice
- ½ oz. Combier Liqueur D'orange
- ¼ oz. agave nectar

1. Salt half the rim of a margarita glass using a lime wedge and Maldon Sea Salt Flakes.
2. Place the cucumber slice in the glass and then fill the glass with ice.
3. Combine the remaining ingredients in a shaker tin, add ice, and shake vigorously.
4. Strain the cocktail into the glass and garnish with a lime wedge.

PALOMA

CONDESA AND EL TECHO
1830 LUDLOW STREET

El Techo commits to the Paloma's signature grapefruit flavor in three ways: a French grapefruit liqueur, fresh grapefruit juice, and a float of pink grapefruit soda. For bartender Stephen Pressman, that triple combination of citrus—and the complexity of reposado tequila—makes for a cocktail that screams summertime in the city.

GLASSWARE: Collins glass
GARNISH: Lime wedge

- 1¾ oz. El Tesoro Reposado Tequila
- 1 oz. grapefruit juice
- ¼ oz. Giffard Crème de Pamplemousse Rose
- ½ oz. fresh lime juice
- ¼ oz. agave nectar
- Fever-Tree Sparkling Pink Grapefruit, to top

1. Combine all of the ingredients, except for the soda, in a cocktail shaker tin.
2. Add ice and shake vigorously until chilled and combined, about 10 seconds.
3. Strain the cocktail into a collins glass filled with fresh ice. Top with the grapefruit soda and garnish with a lime wedge.

SIAM SPRITZ

SAMPAN
124 SOUTH 13TH STREET

For the Siam Spritz, the Sampan bar team wanted to make a cocktail using a tea-infused spirit. They decided on gin and jasmine, as they have a natural affinity. Jasmine was first brought to China from Southeast Asia, so there is a historical connection for Sampan as a Southeast Asian restaurant. Jasmine gin works well in a spritz, a collins, or a sour.

GLASSWARE: Wineglass
GARNISH: Lemon wheel, cucumber spear

- 1½ oz. Jasmine Tea–Infused Gin (see recipe)
- ¼ oz. Cocchi Americano
- ¾ oz. fresh lemon juice
- ¾ oz. Simple Syrup (see recipe on page 11)
- Splash club soda, to top

1. Combine all of the ingredients, except for the club soda, in a cocktail shaker filled with ice and shake until well chilled, about 10 seconds.
2. Strain the cocktail over ice into a wineglass and top with club soda.
3. Garnish with a lemon wheel and a cucumber spear.

JASMINE TEA–INFUSED GIN: In a container, combine 8½ oz. gin and 4 grams jasmine tea, and allow the infusion to sit for 1 hour. Strain.

SEADOG

PEARL AND MARY OYSTER BAR
114 SOUTH 13TH STREET

Evoking summer days by the shore, the Seadog shares much of its DNA with the classic Salty Dog cocktail. Instead of the typical vodka or gin, Pearl and Mary Oyster Bar pairs grapefruit juice with fino sherry. It's lighter on alcohol and brings a delicate floral and nutty flavor profile to the final product. An aromatic rosemary simple syrup ties everything together.

GLASSWARE: Tumbler
GARNISH: Rosemary sprig

- **Salt, for the rim**
- **1 oz. grapefruit juice**
- **¾ oz. fino sherry**
- **¼ oz. Rosemary Simple Syrup (see recipe)**
- **3 drops Saline Solution (see recipe on page 11)**
- **2 oz. Fever-Tree Sparkling Pink Grapefruit**

1. Dip the rim of a tumbler in water then dip the glass in salt to give it a rim.
2. Combine the remaining ingredients, except for the grapefruit soda, in a cocktail shaker with ice and shake hard.
3. Strain the cocktail into the rimmed tumbler over fresh ice and garnish with a rosemary sprig. Top with the soda.

ROSEMARY SIMPLE SYRUP: In a pot over medium heat, combine 200 grams water, 200 grams sugar, and 20 grams fresh rosemary and simmer for 5 minutes.

10TH STREET STRETCH

W PHILADELPHIA
1439 CHESTNUT STREET

Beverage director Isai Xolalpa came to Philadelphia in the summer of 2024. He quickly found himself exploring Philadelphia's diverse food scene, looking for ways to connect with the city through its international influences. "The menu is like a blank paper where I can design and draw whatever I feel like," he says. The 10th Street Stretch is a fusion of Mexican and Asian cultures, pairing mezcal with the savory elements of red miso and a red pimento pepper and radish juice.

GLASSWARE: Nick & Nora glass
GARNISH: Dehydrated hibiscus

- 1 oz. Del Maguey Vida Clásico
- ¾ oz. Red Miso (see recipe)
- ¾ oz. Ginger Juice (see recipe)
- ¾ oz. Red Pimento & Radish Juice (see recipe)
- ¾ oz. Simple Syrup (see recipe on page 11)

1. Combine all of the ingredients in a cocktail shaker with ice and shake until frothy.
2. Double-strain the cocktail into a Nick & Nora.
3. Garnish with dehydrated hibiscus

RED MISO: In a pot over medium-high heat, combine 100 ml red miso and 1 liter water and bring the mixture to a boil. Reduce the heat and simmer for 15 minutes. Double-strain the miso and let it cool.

RED PIMENTO & RADISH JUICE: Remove the stem and carefully remove the seeds from 1 large red pimento pepper. Combine the pepper, 1 radish, and 1 quart water in a blender and blend until smooth. Strain.

GINGER JUICE: Peel 3 to 4 pieces of ginger and cut them into small pieces. Place the ginger in a blender with 1 quart water. Blend until smooth, then strain.

ITALIAN MARKET ESPRESSO MARTINI

W PHILADELPHIA
1439 CHESTNUT STREET

This Espresso Martini is instantly recognizable for its garnish—a cannoli supplied by Isgro's Pastries in the Italian Market. The cocktail, ever trending with guests, has become a mainstay on the W Philadelphia menu. A base of high-quality vodka is supplemented with locally produced amaro, as well as both chocolate and coffee liqueur.

GLASSWARE: Nick & Nora glass
GARNISH: Coffee beans, Isgro's cannoli, dash coffee oil

- 2 oz. espresso
- 1 oz. MLH Distillery Coffee Liqueur
- 1 oz. Grey Goose Vodka
- ½ oz. Vigo Amaro
- ½ oz. MLH Distillery Chocolate Liqueur

1. Combine all of the ingredients in a cocktail shaker with ice and shake continuously until a foam forms and you feel the tin frost.
2. Double-strain the cocktail into a Nick & Nora.
3. Garnish with 3 coffee beans, an Isgro's cannoli, and a dash of coffee oil.

DERANGED LUMBERJACK OLD FASHIONED

BOTLD MIDTOWN
117 SOUTH 13TH STREET

The Deranged Lumberjack Old Fashioned is made with two spirits unique to BOTLD Pennsylvania. The innovative shop specializes in proprietary and exclusive imports, making for a unique shopping and imbibing experience. This cocktail's name is a subtle nod to Philadelphia Eagles sports legend Jason Kelce, and the cocktail uses a Pennsylvania-sourced maple syrup, Sapsquatch. The recipe comes courtesy of beverage manager Roland Coggin.

GLASSWARE: Rocks glass
GARNISH: Orange twist and Amarena cherry on a skewer

- 2 oz. Pigeon Foot Single Barrel Bourbon Whiskey
- ¼ oz. Sapsquatch Organic Maple Syrup
- ¼ oz. Myris Nutmeg Liqueur
- 2 dashes Regans' Orange Bitters No. 6
- Dash Angostura bitters

1. Build all of the ingredients in a mixing glass filled two-thirds of the way with ice.
2. Stir for 8 seconds. Strain the cocktail over a large ice cube into a rocks glass.
3. Express an orange zest over the glass, wrap it around an Amarena cherry, and skewer them to garnish.

FREE BIRD (NA)

HARP AND CROWN
1525 SANSOM STREET

Two types of nonalcoholic spirits come together in place of rum and Campari in this take on the Jungle Bird. Fresh pineapple and lime juice round out the fruity and slightly bitter sipper. It's one of several cocktail alternatives served at Harp and Crown gastropub and a simple way to enjoy a spirit-free drink at home.

GLASSWARE: Rocks glass
GARNISH: Dehydrated lime wheel

- 1½ oz. Caleño Light and Zesty Non-Alcoholic Spirit
- ½ oz. Demerara Syrup (see recipe on page 11)
- ¾ oz. Wilfred's Non-Alcoholic Aperitif
- ¾ oz. fresh pineapple juice
- ½ oz. fresh lime juice

1. Combine all of the ingredients in a cocktail shaker with ice and shake until chilled and combined, about 10 seconds.
2. Strain the cocktail into a rocks glass with fresh ice.
3. Garnish with a dehydrated lime wheel.

HAYMAKER

ENSWELL
1528 SPRUCE STREET

Credit to Vince Stipo, the Haymaker is Enswell's version of an Espresso Martini. This cocktail gets a bold twist thanks to the cafe's relationship with Rival Bros Coffee (Enswell serves its own espresso in the restaurant). The drink is served on the rocks instead of up and made with whiskey instead of vodka. It also includes nuts in the form of orgeat syrup. Enswell's licensing means it uses spirits exclusively from local New Liberty Distillery, but any quality options available will do. You can substitute very strong coffee or cold brew concentrate for the espresso.

GLASSWARE: Rocks glass
GARNISH: Instant coffee, Maldon Sea Salt Flakes

- 1 oz. orgeat
- ¾ oz. espresso
- ¾ oz. New Liberty Distillery Liberty Belle Coffee Liqueur
- ¾ oz. New Liberty Distillery Kinsey Whiskey
- 1 oz. Vanilla Coffee Cream (see recipe), to top

1. Chill a large rocks glass. Combine all of the ingredients, except for the cream, in a cocktail shaker and shake vigorously for 5 seconds.
2. Strain the cocktail into the chilled glass over 4 large cubes.
3. Top with the cream and garnish with a smattering of instant coffee and a fleck or two of Maldon Sea Salt Flakes.

VANILLA COFFEE CREAM. In the metal bowl of an electric mixer, combine 4 oz. heavy whipping cream, 1 tablespoon powdered sugar, ¼ teaspoon vanilla paste, and ½ teaspoon instant coffee. Beat until soft peaks form. Transfer to a storage vessel and chill until ready to use.

FRENCH BREAKFAST

BAR LESIEUR
1523 SANSOM STREET

Bar Lesieur is restaurateur Michael Schulson's tribute to modern French cooking. With the French Breakfast, beverage director Michael McCaulley drew inspiration from two modern cocktail classics: the Breakfast Martini and the London Fog. The signature element in this aromatic Gin Sour is the French breakfast tea simple syrup, made with tea sourced from Mariage Frères in Paris.

GLASSWARE: Coupe glass
GARNISH: Dehydrated lemon wheel, lemon oil spritz

- 1½ oz. gin
- ¾ oz. French Breakfast Tea Simple Syrup (see recipe)
- 1 oz. egg white
- ¾ oz. fresh lemon juice
- Barspoon orange marmalade

1. Chill a coupe glass. Combine all of the ingredients in a mixing tin and dry-shake (no ice) to foam the egg white.
2. Add ice, shake again, vigorously, and strain the cocktail into the chilled coupe.
3. Garnish with dehydrated lemon wheel and spray with lemon oil.

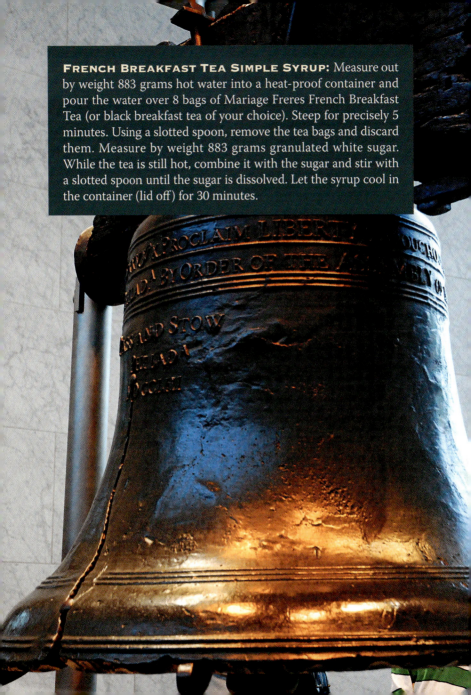

FRENCH BREAKFAST TEA SIMPLE SYRUP: Measure out by weight 883 grams hot water into a heat-proof container and pour the water over 8 bags of Mariage Freres French Breakfast Tea (or black breakfast tea of your choice). Steep for precisely 5 minutes. Using a slotted spoon, remove the tea bags and discard them. Measure by weight 883 grams granulated white sugar. While the tea is still hot, combine it with the sugar and stir with a slotted spoon until the sugar is dissolved. Let the syrup cool in the container (lid off) for 30 minutes.

MARGARITA VERT

BAR LESIEUR
1523 SANSOM STREET

In keeping with Bar Lesieur's French influence, beverage director Michael McCaulley crafted this green-hued take on a Margarita. It gets its character from the herbaceous and botanical notes of génépy, an aromatic liqueur from the Alps region of France. The rest of the alcohol base is a fifty-fifty split of smoky mezcal and blanco tequila. Fresh lime juice and a basil leaf garnish round out this colorful European riff on a classic.

GLASSWARE: Rocks glass
GARNISH: Basil leaf

- Lavender Salt (see recipe), for the rim
- 1 oz. Banhez Mezcal
- 1 oz. blanco tequila
- ½ oz. Dolin Génépy le Chamois Liqueur
- ¾ oz. fresh lime juice
- ½ oz. Agave Simple Syrup (see recipe)
- 4 dashes Scrappy's Fire Tincture

1. Prepare a rocks glass with a lavender salt rim.
2. Combine the remaining ingredients in a cocktail shaker with ice and shake well until chilled, about 10 seconds.
3. Strain the cocktail into the rimmed rocks glass over a large rock of ice.
4. Garnish with a basil leaf.

Lavender Salt: Using a mortar and pestle, grind 1 tablespoon dried lavender flowers into a powder. Add sea salt, as needed, and mix.

Agave Simple Syrup: In a saucepan over medium-low heat, gently heat 1 cup agave nectar and 1 cup water. Stir until combined—do not boil. Let the syrup cool before using.

PERSIAN PALOMA

DEAR DAPHNI
125 SOUTH 20TH STREET

The Schulson Collective is known for its globe-trotting restaurants, and Dear Daphni brings a taste of the Mediterranean region to City Center. The bar menu includes this Persian Paloma, which beverage guru Michael McCaulley mixes using a house grenadine syrup and two types of tequila. A za'atar salt rim lends each sip an earthy, spicy, and tangy complement to the Paloma's distinctive grapefruit bite.

GLASSWARE: Collins glass
GARNISH: Rosemary sprig, charred grapefruit slice

- Za'atar Salt (see recipe), for the rim
- 1¼ oz. blanco tequila
- ½ oz. Dear Daphni House Grenadine (see recipe)
- ¾ oz. reposado tequila
- ½ oz. fresh lime juice
- 3 dashes grapefruit bitters
- 3 oz. grapefruit soda, to top

1. Combine all of the ingredients, except for the soda, in a cocktail shaker tin.
2. Rim a collins glass with the Za'atar Salt and fill the glass with ice.
3. Fill the shaker tin with ice and shake hard for about 10 seconds.
4. Strain the cocktail into the rimmed collins glass.
5. Top with grapefruit soda, and garnish with a rosemary sprig and a charred ruby red grapefruit slice.

Za'atar Salt: Combine salt and za'atar at a 4:1 ratio (4 teaspoons salt, 1 teaspoon za'atar, for example).

Dear Daphni House Grenadine: In a medium saucepan over medium heat, combine 250 grams pomegranate juice, 250 grams sugar, 1 oz. pomegranate molasses, and 3 grams orange blossom water and stir until all of the ingredients are dissolved (do not boil). Remove from heat and let the grenadine cool before storing.

DONE AND DUSTED

CHARLIE WAS A SINNER
131 SOUTH 13TH STREET

The Done and Dusted has kept its place on Charlie Was a Sinner's cocktail menu since opening day. The Espresso Martini spin, created by bartender Robert Caskey, is unique in its homemade coconut-based crème liqueur that gets amped up with cocoa, brandy, and espresso from Philadelphia producer La Colombe. Tequila reposado and coffee liqueur accent the caramel backbone and nuttiness of this delightful dessert drink.

GLASSWARE: Coupe glass
GARNISH: Cocoa Blend (see recipe)

- 1½ oz. cream liqueur (see recipe)
- 1¼ oz Caffè Borghetti
- ¾ oz. reposado tequila

1. Combine all of the ingredients in a cocktail shaker and shake with ice until chilled.
2. Strain the cocktail into a coupe and dust the top of the cocktail with the Cocoa Blend.

Cocoa Blend: Combine equal parts salt, cocoa powder, and ground espelette pepper and mix well.

SIP YOUR SINS

CHARLIE WAS A SINNER
131 SOUTH 13TH STREET

This tiki sipper incorporates bourbon and rum, two spirits that have a rich history in the American cocktail culture. At Charlie Was a Sinner, it's powered by the oak and subtle sweetness of a special Knob Creek Barrel Select, crafted specifically for the bar in partnership with the distillery. The cocktail is credited to beverage manager Drew Young, and the bar serves it, garnish and all, in a tiki tumbler designed by Felt+Fat.

GLASSWARE: Tiki mug

GARNISH: Fresh mint sprigs, pineapple wedge, brûléed banana slice, cinnamon stick, 2 dashes Angostura bitters

- 1¼ oz. pineapple juice
- ¾ oz. Knob Creek Single Barrel Select Bourbon
- ¾ oz. blackstrap rum
- ¾ oz. Giffard Banane du Brésil
- ¼ oz. Clément Créole Shrubb Orange Liqueur
- ½ oz. fresh lime juice
- 2 dashes Angostura bitters
- Club soda or ginger beer, to top

1. Combine all of the ingredients, except for the bitters and soda, in a cocktail shaker filled with ice and shake until chilled, 10 to 15 seconds.
2. Strain the cocktail over fresh cracked ice in a tiki mug. Top with club soda or ginger beer for a spicier finish.
3. Garnish with fresh mint sprigs, pineapple wedge, brûléed banana slice, cinnamon stick, and 2 dashes Angostura bitters.

AWAJI-MUSUBI

DOUBLE KNOT
120 SOUTH 13TH STREET

The Awaji-Musubi is named after the Japanese ceremonial knot traditionally used in weddings. Double Knot bartender Chris Serpentine characterizes this cocktail, with its whisky base and plum wine float, as a playful twist on a New York Sour. The small amount of Byrrh Grand Quinquina aperitif adds subtle bitter and earthy undertones.

GLASSWARE: Rocks glass
GARNISH: Plum wine float, cherry on a skewer

- 1½ oz. Suntory Whisky Toki
- ¾ oz. fresh lemon juice
- ½ oz. Byrrh Grand Quinquina aperitif
- ½ oz. Demarara Syrup (see recipe on page 11)
- 1 egg white
- ½ oz. Choya plum wine

1. Combine all of the ingredients except the Choya plum wine into a cocktail tin filled with ice.
2. Shake well until chilled and combined.
3. Strain into a rocks glass with fresh ice.
4. Garnish with a cherry and float with plum wine.

TOM BRANDER, WILDER

Tom Brander is the beverage manager of Wilder.

How did you get started in bartending?

I started in the restaurant industry as a busser at a local brewery in West Chester. I moved up to server there, and another local bar hired me as a bouncer/barback. I actually was barbacking for my brother, who taught me to bartend. Meanwhile at the brewery, I became involved in the production side, being brought in as an assistant brewer. I then started bartending at the brewery in addition to brewing. As far as getting into craft cocktails, it took the Covid furlough to move me from the brewery to take a job at a local restaurant. There, my friend taught me the craft side of things, as she had spent the majority of her career in Philadelphia.

What do you enjoy most about bartending?

Some of my favorite aspects of bartending are the creativity and overall hospitality you get. It is a different experience being behind the bar versus serving. With bartending, you have the ability to truly craft the experience for your guest from start to finish. Being behind the bar allows the guest to come into your environment, and they are usually there for that experience.

What tips and tricks do you have for home bartenders? Is there a secret to making a great cocktail?

My top tips for creating cocktails are to always think of your ingredients as a whole. Through this, you can make sure the things are balanced. Liqueurs have an inherent sweetness that needs to be balanced by the presence of acidity. Salt can bring this sweetness down as well. On that note, salt and pepper are hugely underrated ingredients in cocktails (the majority of my syrups use at least one kind of peppercorn). Finally, I would say never be afraid to think outside the box. Some of my best cocktails come from just saying, "Let's just try it out and see what happens."

What do you enjoy most about the Philadelphia cocktail community?

I love the cocktail community in Philadelphia. There are many creative and talented people in this city, and I think we are finally receiving recognition on a more national scale. One thing I always talk about when it comes to the hospitality and restaurant community as a whole in Philadelphia is the collaboration. I find it so helpful to be able to turn to my fellow bartenders when it comes to working on new drinks. Countless times I have reached out after trying a cocktail somewhere to find out the specific details. This has also happened with people reaching out after coming to Wilder. Everyone is always happy to provide recipes or tips on how to achieve the end goal. This city is definitely a force to be reckoned with, and it is exciting to be part of it for the future.

THE BUTCHER

WILDER
2009 SANSOM STREET

Beverage manager Tom Brander stumbled into this recipe by chance, having overheard a random description of another drink by one of the servers at Wilder. The final product is a sipper that blends various spirits and liqueurs, including Armagnac, a style of French brandy that can be tough to tame in cocktails.

GLASSWARE: Mini coupe glass

- 1 oz. Chateau de Pellehaut Reserve Tenareze Armagnac
- 1 oz. Yellow Chartreuse
- ½ oz. Maggie's Farm Falernum Liqueur
- ½ oz. Lazzaroni Amaretto
- 3 dashes Peychaud's bitters
- 2 dashes Regans' Orange Bitters No. 6
- 1 lemon peel, expressed

1. Combine all of the ingredients, except for the lemon peel, in a mixing glass with ice.
2. Stir well until combined and chilled.
3. Strain the cocktail into a mini coupe. Rub the rim of the glass with a lemon peel and discard the peel.

KIMONO RACER

WILDER
2009 SANSOM STREET

This cocktail takes its inspiration from the increasingly popular use of shrubs in cocktails.

GLASSWARE: Nick & Nora glass
GARNISH: Szechuan Pickle (see recipe)

- ½ oz. Askur Gin
- ½ oz. Balsamic Syrup (see recipe)
- ½ oz. Oka Kura Yuzu Liqueur
- ½ oz. fresh lemon juice
- Prosecco, to top

1. Combine all of the ingredients, except for the prosecco, in a cocktail tin with ice and shake well, until chilled and combined.

2. Double-strain the cocktail into a Nick & Nora.

3. Top with prosecco and garnish with a Szechuan pickle.

BALSAMIC SYRUP: In a pot over medium-low heat, toast 20 grams Szechuan peppercorns until fragrant. Add 1 cup water, 1 cup balsamic vinegar, and 2 cups sugar and simmer for 5 minutes. Strain and let cool.

SZECHUAN PICKLES: Fill a Cambro or other kitchen storage container with 500 grams rice vinegar, 375 grams filtered cold water, 15 grams sesame oil, 15 grams crushed Szechuan peppercorns, 30 grams garlic, thinly sliced, 15 grams MSG, 50 grams sugar, and 50 grams salt and mix. Crinkle-cut English cucumbers and submerge them in the liquid mixture for at least 24 hours.

JILLIAN MOORE, MY LOUP

Jillian Moore is the head bartender at My Loup.

How did you get started in bartending?

I have been working in restaurants since I was fifteen and got my start in bartending when I was twenty-two, at a martini bar in Ocean City, Maryland, for a summer after college.

What do you enjoy most about bartending?

I think a lot about a passage I read in Gary Regan's *Joy of Mixology* about mindful bartending. To sum it up, anyone can learn how to make drinks fast. Success behind the bar for some is more about understanding the people they serve, to make guests feel the presence of the bartender as a person, rather than just serving a function. I take having a good time very seriously and doing that mindfully is the best part of my job. I enjoy making people feel seen as I show them a good time.

What tips and tricks do you have for home bartenders? Is there a secret to making a great cocktail?

That's a hard question for me to answer. I think most people would say good product, ice, or fresh ingredients—and that is definitely true in some cases—but then I think about the times when you don't have those things available. What makes the quality of a drink in those circumstances? I think quality is often more about how the drink is enjoyed, whether alone or with people.

AGAVE VESPER

MY LOUP
2005 WALNUT STREET

At My Loup, bar director Jillian Moore focuses on classic recipes that complement the kitchen's frequently changing seasonal menu. She says that the Agave Vesper debuted on the menu shortly after the restaurant's opening and is unlikely to ever leave. Moore especially enjoys combing through old bartending books to find opportunities to swap tequila and mezcal into recipes where whiskey or gin would have traditionally been used.

GLASSWARE: Martini glass
GARNISH: Lemon peel, expressed

- 1¾ oz. Siembra Valles Tequila Blanco
- ½ oz. Mezcal Vago Elote
- ½ oz. Cocchi Americano
- ¼ oz. Giffard Banane du Brésil

1. Chill a martini glass. Combine all of the ingredients in a cocktail mixer with ice.
2. Stir well until chilled and combined.
3. Strain the cocktail into the chilled martini glass.
4. Express a lemon peel over the drink, then cut the peel to an oval, and a slit to pinch along the rim, then add the peel as a garnish.

SACRIFICE TO THE GODS

A.BAR
1737 WALNUT STREET

Bar manager Harry Jamison describes this drink as a cross between a Dark 'n' Stormy and an Espresso Tonic. The bitterness of Averna amaro is balanced by two housemade syrups—one made from spiced coffee and one made from ginger—for a rich texture and surprisingly savory flavor. The drink's name comes from the steep price Jamison's handyman jokingly placed on fixing a broken ice machine.

GLASSWARE: Highball glass
GARNISH: Mint sprig, orange twist

- 1½ oz. Amaro Averna
- ½ oz. Planteray O.F.T.D. Overproof Rum
- ½ oz. Spiced Coffee Syrup (see recipe)
- ¾ oz. fresh lime juice
- ¼ oz. Ginger Syrup (see recipe)
- Fever-Tree Premium Indian Tonic Water, to top

1. Combine all of the ingredients, except for the tonic water, in a cocktail shaker filled with ice.
2. Shake well, until chilled and combined.
3. Strain the cocktail into a highball with an ice spear, and top with tonic water.
4. Garnish with a mint sprig and an orange twist.

Ginger Syrup: In a saucepan over low heat, combine 2 oz. white sugar and 1 oz. fresh ginger juice (2:1 ratio by weight). Simmer the mixture on low, stirring, until the sugar is dissolved. Allow the syrup to cool.

Spiced Coffee Syrup: In a container, whisk together Rich Demerara Simple Syrup (see recipe on page 11) juniper berries, black peppercorns, and 1½ oz. Trablit 1845 Liquid Coffee Extract. Strain.

NECK BRACE

A.BAR
1737 WALNUT STREET

Bartender Jacob Fusco named this cocktail after the Ratatat song that the team at a.bar listened to when a night of service reached its most chaotic phase. The drink takes on punchy flavors of a Rum Daiquiri, but its preparation, stirred with a lime cordial rather than shaken with lime juice, brings out a silky texture.

GLASSWARE: Rocks glass
GARNISH: Dehydrated lime wheel

- 1½ oz. Foursquare Probitas White Blended Rum
- ½ oz. Lime Cordial (see recipe)
- ½ oz. Tempus Fugit Crème de Banane
- ¼ oz. Salers Gentian Apéritif
- ¼ oz. Smith & Cross Jamaica Rum
- 3 dashes Angostura bitters
- 3 dashes Bittermens 'Elemakule Tiki Bitters

1. Combine all of the ingredients in a mixing glass with ice.
2. Stir well until combined and chilled.
3. Strain the cocktail over a big rock of ice and garnish with a dehydrated lime wheel.

LIME CORDIAL: Combine 500 grams white sugar, 450 grams hot water, 3 oz. lime juice, and 1½ oz. citric acid in a blender, such as a Vitamix, and blend until incorporated.

BOMBAY MOON

1 TIPPLING PLACE
2006 CHESTNUT STREET

Throughout the years, the team at 1 Tippling Place has made two trips to India, opening a pop-up bar in Mumbai. This Old Fashioned variation has long held strong as the favorite of its Indian-inspired cocktails due to its simplicity and authentic flavors. Lead bartender Chris Zingler makes Masala syrup from scratch, using green cardamom, black peppercorn, clove, fennel, coriander, and ginger root. At home, you can make a faster version with your favorite masala chai tea bags. As the drink slowly dilutes, notice the tea flavors begin to outshine the bourbon. It's a journey in a glass.

GLASSWARE: Rocks glass
GARNISH: Orange peel, flamed

- 2 oz. bourbon
- ¼ oz. Masala Chai Syrup (see recipe)
- 2 dashes Angostura bitters

1. Combine all of the ingredients in a large rocks glass.
2. Add a 2-inch cube of ice, stir a few times, and garnish with a flamed orange peel.

MASALA CHAI SYRUP: Preheat the oven to 350°F. Lightly crush 12 green cardamom pods and ½ teaspoon black peppercorns and set them aside. Toast ½ teaspoon whole cloves, ½ teaspoon whole coriander, 1 teaspoon fennel seed, 1 cinnamon stick, and 3 tablespoons chopped ginger root in the oven until aromatic. In a saucepan, combine the spices with 1 cup sugar and 1 cup water and bring to a boil while stirring. Remove the syrup from heat and allow the mixture to steep for 10 minutes. Strain and store in the refrigerator.

RASPBERRY LYCHEE BELLINI

SKYHIGH LOUNGE
ONE NORTH 19TH STREET

The elegant, bubbly cocktail comes from the team at the SkyHigh Lounge, located on the sixtieth floor of the Four Seasons Hotel. Its elegance is a fitting match for the bar's panoramic views of downtown Philadelphia. The wallet-friendly Crémant de Bourgogne can be easily swapped for a sparkling wine of choice.

GLASSWARE: Champagne flute
GARNISH: Edible flower

- 2 oz. Raspberry Lychee Base (see recipe)
- 4 oz. Crémant de Bourgogne, to top

1. Fill a champagne flute with Raspberry Lychee Base.
2. Top with Crémant de Bourgogne sparkline wine.
3. Garnish with an edible flower

RASPBERRY LYCHEE BASE: In a blender, combine 400 grams frozen lychee puree, defrosted; 45 grams fresh raspberries; 15 grams elderflower cordial; and 10 grams fresh lime juice and blend until smooth. Pass the mixture through a chinois or fine-mesh strainer.

GINGER MARGARITA

SKYHIGH LOUNGE
ONE NORTH 19TH STREET

SkyHigh Lounge is the place to find luxury twists on classic cocktails. This spicy-sweet Margarita gets an extra depth of flavor by using an añejo tequila base instead of the typical silver variety. On the outside of the glass, the usual salt rim gets reimagined with toasted fresh ginger and kosher salt and provides an extra kick that should not be overlooked.

GLASSWARE: Rocks glass
GARNISH: Lime wedge

- **Ginger Salt (see recipe), for the rim**
- **¾ oz. Ginger Lime Syrup (see recipe)**
- **1½ oz. Dulce Vida Añejo Tequila**
- **½ oz. Cointreau**
- **½ oz. fresh lime juice**

1. Wet the rim of a rocks glass with a lime wedge then dip the glass in the Ginger Salt to give it a rim.
2. Combine the remaining ingredients in a cocktail shaker filled with ice and shake.
3. Strain the cocktail into the rimmed rocks glass with fresh ice.
4. Garnish with a lime wedge.

GINGER SALT: Preheat the oven to 170°F. Spread ginger pulp, as needed, on a silicone baking sheet (Silpat) or parchment paper and place the sheet in the oven until it is very dry. Using a blender or food processor, grind the dried ginger pulp into a powder. Weigh the ginger powder and combine it with kosher salt at a ratio of 1:1.

GINGER LIME SYRUP: In a pot over medium-low heat, combine 1 cup lime juice and 1 cup sugar. Bring the mixture to a simmer and immediately remove from heat. Place 30 grams fresh ginger, sliced and pureed, in a bain-marie (or shallow baking pan), pour the lime-sugar syrup over it, and allow the mixture to cool to room temperature. Strain through a chinois, pushing for total extraction and reserving the ginger pulp for the Ginger Salt.

ASTRONAUT

THE CONTINENTAL MIDTOWN
1801 CHESTNUT STREET

Opened in 2004, The Continental Midtown was restaurateur Stephen Starr's first restaurant project. Twenty years later, the menu of global tapas and Martinis continues to draw crowds. The Astronaut walks along the boundary of the Martini formula, using peach vodka, triple sec, and a "cosmic sherbet" made with orange juice and Tang powder.

GLASSWARE: Coupe glass

- **Edible gold glitter, for the rim**
- **Tang, for the rim**
- **1½ oz. Peachka Vodka**
- **1 oz. Cosmic Sherbet (see recipe)**
- **1 oz. Sour AF Lemon Juice**
- **½ oz. triple sec**

1. Chill a coupe glass. Wet the rim of the coupe and then dip the glass in edible gold glitter and Tang powder to give it a rim.

2. Combine all of the ingredients in a cocktail shaker with ice and shake until chilled and combined.

3. Strain the cocktail into the chilled coupe.

COSMIC SHERBET: In a large kitchen storage container, combine 12 oz. white sugar, 8 oz. orange juice, 4 oz. water, 2½ teaspoons Tang powder, and a pinch of edible gold glitter and whisk until the sugar is completely dissolved. Transfer the mixture to an airtight container and refrigerate before use.

FROZEN BLOOD ORANGE MARGARITA

EL VEZ
121 SOUTH 13TH STREET

The recipe for this frozen Margarita is designed to be shared between a few friends. All it requires is some freezer space and a good blender. The combination of blood orange, orange, cranberry, and fresh lime juice give it an impressive color and a bright, citrusy finish. Be sure to enjoy it soon after blending to maintain the best possible consistency.

GLASSWARE: Margarita glass

- 10 oz. blood orange juice
- 5 oz. blanco tequila
- 4 oz. orange juice
- 4 oz. cranberry juice
- 2 oz. triple sec
- 1½ oz. fresh lime juice
- 1 oz. Simple Syrup (see recipe on page 11)

1. Combine all of the ingredients in a large container and mix well, then pour the cocktail into ice cube trays and freeze.
2. Add the frozen cubes to a blender and blend quickly until smooth.

FELIPE COLLINS

EL VEZ
121 SOUTH 13TH STREET

Flashy, trendy, and full of energy describe El Vez. Agave takes the spotlight behind the bar of this high-end Mexican restaurant—for good reason. El Vez serves its fair share of Margaritas, but for something different, try this shaken mix of blanco tequila and chile liqueur. Fresh lemon juice and a touch of honey balance the spice.

GLASSWARE: Collins glass

- 1½ oz. Espolòn Tequila Blanco
- 1 oz. Ancho Reyes Verde Chile Poblano Liqueur
- ¾ oz. fresh lemon juice
- ¾ oz. honey

1. Combine all of the ingredients in a cocktail shaker with ice and shake well, until chilled and combined.
2. Strain the cocktail into a collins glass filled with fresh ice.

BP MANHATTAN

BARCLAY PRIME
237 SOUTH 18TH STREET

The sophistication of a classic Manhattan is a natural companion for a red meat dinner. Just as Barclay Prime brightens up the traditional steak house, so does its namesake cocktail for the traditional cocktail. The secret ingredient in this rye whiskey sipper is a tobacco-infused white vermouth.

GLASSWARE: Martini glass
GARNISH: Luxardo cherry, orange peel

- 2 oz. Sagamore Spirit Rye Whiskey
- 1 oz. Tobacco-Infused White Vermouth (see recipe)
- ½ oz. Amaro Nardini

1. Combine all of the ingredients in a cocktail mixing glass with ice.
2. Stir well, until chilled and combined.
3. Strain the cocktail into a martini glass and garnish with a Luxardo cherry and an orange peel.

TOBACCO-INFUSED WHITE VERMOUTH: In a large kitchen storage container, combine 1 (750 ml) bottle of Dolin Blanc Vermouth and 1 tin of Cult Blood Red Moon pipe tobacco and steep for 24 hours. Strain and rebottle.

SPRITZ ROYALE

PARC
227 SOUTH 18TH STREET

Parc is peak Parisian elegance in the heart of Philadelphia. The Spritz Royale makes a fine companion to kick off a meal, whether it's a leisurely brunch or celebratory dinner. This take on the Aperol Spritz goes in a grapefruit direction, with liqueur and fresh juice.

GLASSWARE: Wineglass
GARNISH: Grapefruit slice

- 1 oz. Aperol
- 1 oz. Combier Crème de Pamplemousse Rose
- 1 oz. grapefruit juice
- ½ oz. fresh lemon juice
- Sparkling water, to top

1. Line a wineglass with a grapefruit slice and then fill the glass with ice.
2. Add all of the ingredients to the glass and top with sparkling water.
3. Garnish with a grapefruit triangle.

OLD FASHIONED

BUTCHER AND SINGER
1500 WALNUT STREET

Old Fashioneds are beloved for their simplicity, and this offering from glamorous Butcher and Singer holds to that standard. House-made Honey Rose Syrup provides a tasteful flourish that respects the philosophy that less is more.

GLASSWARE: Rocks glass
GARNISH: Lemon twist

- 2 oz. Knob Creek 7 Year Old Rye Whiskey
- 1 oz. Honey Rose Syrup (see recipe)
- Dash Angostura bitters
- Dash Regans' Orange Bitters No. 6

1. Combine all of the ingredients in a mixing glass with ice and stir well, until chilled and combined.
2. Strain the cocktail into a rocks glass over a large ice cube.
3. Garnish with a lemon twist.

HONEY ROSE SYRUP: In a pot or saucepan over medium-low heat, combine 1 cup water, 1 cup honey, and 1½ teaspoons rosewater. Gently heat and stir until all the ingredients are combined.

INVESTMENT MANHATTAN

BUTCHER AND SINGER
1500 WALNUT STREET

In this well-rounded, elegant Manhattan recipe, a healthy pour of rye whiskey is accompanied by sherry, Grand Marnier, and cherry liqueur—no vermouth required. It's no guaranteed predictor of business success, but it's a good bet.

GLASSWARE: Martini glass
GARNISH: Orange peel

- 1½ oz. rye whiskey
- ¾ oz. Williams & Humbert Dry Sack Medium Dry Sherry
- ½ oz. Grand Marnier Cordon Rouge
- ½ oz. Heering Cherry Liqueur
- 3 dashes Angostura bitters

1. Combine all of the ingredients in a mixing glass filled with ice.
2. Stir well until chilled, about 10 seconds.
3. Strain the cocktail into a martini glass and garnish with an orange peel.

PIMM'S DELUXE

THE DANDELION
124 SOUTH 18TH STREET

The Dandelion brings the charm of an English pub to Philadelphia. It's no surprise, then, that it has served this version of the Pimm's Cup from the beginning. Pimm's is a bitter, fruity, and herbal liqueur, traditionally paired up with a London dry gin, lemon, and ginger ale for a refreshing highball. The Dandelion takes a bit of a detour, incorporating muddled cucumbers and serving it like a Martini—up and without the fizz.

GLASSWARE: Coupe glass
GARNISH: Cucumber slice

- ½ oz. sliced cucumbers
- 1 oz. Pimm's
- 1 oz. London dry gin
- ¾ oz. fresh lemon juice
- ¾ oz. Simple Syrup (see recipe on page 11)

1. In a cocktail mixing tin, muddle the sliced cucumbers.
2. Add ice, then add the remaining ingredients and shake well until combined and chilled, about 10 to 15 seconds.
3. Strain the cocktail into a coupe and garnish with a cucumber slice.

PIÑA COLADA

BOLO
2025 SANSOM STREET

The Piña Colada became Puerto Rico's national drink in 1978. Since then, locals and tourists alike have enjoyed the beverage and its simple formula of coconut cream, pineapple juice, and rum. At Bolo, chef Yun Fuentes and his team honor their Puerto Rican roots by proudly serving Piña Colada in several ways. This recipe is the way Bolo makes its classic Piña Colada.

GLASSWARE: Hurricane glass
GARNISH: 2 pineapple fronds, pineapple wedge, 3 skewered Luxardo cherries

- 2 oz. Bolo's Coconut Cream (see recipe)
- 2 oz. pineapple juice
- 2 oz. Don Q Gold

1. Combine coconut cream, pineapple juice, and rum with 2 cups ice cubes in a blender and blend until smooth.
2. Pour the cocktail into a hurricane glass and garnish with 2 pineapple fronds, a pineapple wedge, and 3 skewered Luxardo cherries and serve with a straw.

BOLO'S COCONUT CREAM: Combine 1 part coconut milk and 1 part Coco López Cream of Coconut and mix until combined.

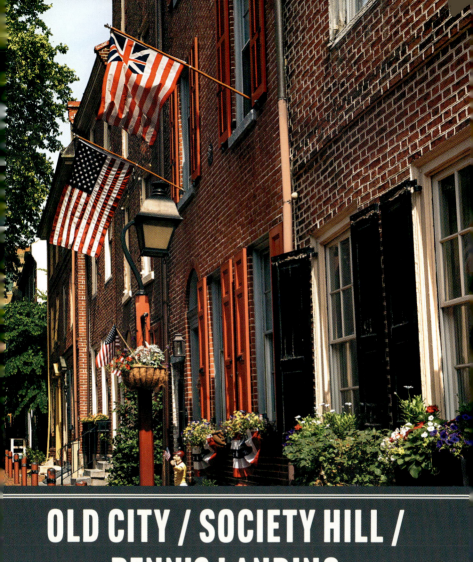

OLD CITY / SOCIETY HILL / PENN'S LANDING

- Beet It
- Pear of Apples
- Classic Mojito
- Paradise Rum Punch
- Bartender for Hire
- Garden Smash
- Midsummer Night
- Islay Roses on Your Grave
- Piña Colobsta
- Les Paul
- Lucky Number
- Strawberry Street
- The Boog
- Rocket Fuel
- Scorched Atlas
- Lemonana
- Limoncello Fresco Spritz

American history echoes across this slice of Philadelphia, the home of the Liberty Bell and also Independence Hall, where both the Declaration of Independence (1776) and the United States Constitution (1787) were signed by America's founding fathers. These adjoining neighborhoods constitute one of the oldest parts of the city, with some of its signature red-brick buildings standing for more than three hundred years. The cocktail scene, by contrast, is as modern as ever. Options include enjoying a drink and a curated playlist at 48 Record Bar, indulging in French-inspired mixology and cooking at Forsythia, or grabbing a classic Mojito at Cuba Libre.

BEET IT

THE MORRIS
225 SOUTH 8TH STREET

The Morris bartender and general manager Christopher Harrop imagined this drink for his Ukrainian fiancée, who eats beets almost daily. After many attempts that "kept tasting like dirt," Harrop remained determined to make the cocktail work. He found that the balance lies in letting the beets (and carrots) steep in gin for no more than four hours. The idea for the tarragon and honey syrup came from his background in French cuisine.

GLASSWARE: Coupe glass
GARNISH: Lemon twist

- 1½ oz. Beet-and-Carrot Gin Infusion (see recipe)
- ¾ oz. Domaine de Canton French Ginger Liqueur
- ½ oz. Honey-Tarragon Syrup (see recipe)
- ½ oz. fresh lemon juice

1. Combine all of the ingredients in a cocktail shaker with ice.
2. Shake well until combined and chilled.
3. Double-strain the cocktail into a coupe glass.
4. Express a lemon twist over the cocktail and set the twist on the glass rim.

BEET-AND-CARROT GIN INFUSION: Peel, wash, and quarter half a beet and half a carrot. Split chopped carrots and beets into two separate quart-sized containers. Divide 1 (750 ml) bottle of Revivalist Garden Gin between the containers. Let the infusions sit for 2 to 4 hours. Strain out and rebottle the gin.

HONEY-TARRAGON SYRUP: In a container, combine 1 cup honey and 1 cup hot water and mix until everything is incorporated. Add 10 grams fresh tarragon and let the mixture sit until the syrup is at room temperature. Strain, date, and store in the refrigerator.

PEAR OF APPLES

THE MORRIS
225 SOUTH 8TH STREET

Hoodie weather, campfires, and all things apple make fall the favorite time of year for Christopher Harrop, bartender and GM at The Morris. He wanted to create a drink that tasted like fall in glass, and he did so by using fresh ingredients. The drink includes two homemade components: a Red Delicious apple cordial and a cider doctored up with poached pears. As he tells the story, Harrop says the mezcal-forward Pear of Apples cocktail was finalized the morning the bar's fall cocktail menu was being rolled out. It's since become a fan favorite.

GLASSWARE: Rocks glass
GARNISH: Cinnamon stick

- 1½ oz. Banhez Mezcal
- ½ oz. Apple Cordial (see recipe)
- ½ oz. fresh lemon juice
- 2 oz. Poached Pear Cider (see recipe)

1. Combine all of the ingredients in a mixing glass with ice and stir.

2. Strain the cocktail over one large ice cube into a rocks glass and garnish with a cinnamon stick.

APPLE CORDIAL: In a pot over medium-high heat, combine 1 Red Delicious apple, quartered and deseeded, and 2 cups coconut water. Bring the mixture to a boil, then reduce to a simmer and simmer for 20 to 30 minutes, or until the water takes on a pink color. Add 1 teaspoon vanilla extract and 300 grams sugar and stir until the sugar is dissolved. Add 3 grams citric acid and stir. Remove the cordial from the heat, allow it to cool, and strain.

POACHED PEAR CIDER: Peel and quarter 3 pears. Put the pear pieces into a pot and add 4 cups apple cider and a cinnamon stick. Bring the mixture to a boil, reduce the heat, and then let simmer on low for 30 minutes. While the mixture simmers, use parchment paper to make a cartouche (a thin layer) over the pot. Remove the mixture from heat and allow it to cool in a heat-proof container, such as a Cambro, for up to 24 hours. Blend, strain, and store the cider.

CLASSIC MOJITO

CUBA LIBRE
10 SOUTH 2ND STREET

Sipping a Mojito is like liquid air-conditioning during the summer months. Cuba Libre serves perhaps the best-known version in the city, offering nine total varieties in addition to the classic build of white rum, mint, sugar, lime, and soda presented here. This recipe calls for fresh-pressed sugarcane juice (*guarapo* in Spanish) in the place of granulated sugar or simple syrup, giving the drink a floral and more nuanced sweetness. For those who don't know, a zombie glass is a tall skinny glass that shows off the mint in this recipe.

GLASSWARE: Zombie glass
GARNISH: Lime wheel

- 2 oz. white rum
- 2½ oz. fresh sugarcane juice
- 1¼ oz. fresh lime juice
- 6 leaves spearmint
- Club soda, to top

1. In a cocktail shaker, combine the rum, sugarcane juice, and lime juice. Tear the spearmint leaves and add them to the shaker.
2. Fill the shaker with ice and shake well, 6 times.
3. Pour the cocktail into a zombie glass. Top with a splash of club soda.
4. Garnish with a lime wheel and serve with a straw.

PARADISE RUM PUNCH

CUBA LIBRE
10 SOUTH 2ND STREET

Two types of rum do the heavy lifting in this crowd-pleasing tropical concoction. A Cuba Libre menu standby, this fan favorite uses fresh juices and liqueurs to create a harmony of sweet, fruity, nutty, and bitter flavors. This is one drink that packs a punch and will satisfy anyone dreaming of warm waters and ocean breezes.

GLASSWARE: Pineapple glass
GARNISH: Orange slice, mint sprig

- 1½ oz. pineapple juice
- 1½ oz. fresh orange juice
- 1 oz. Don Q Coco
- ¾ oz. Don Q Gold
- ¾ oz. Licor 43
- ¾ oz. fresh sugarcane juice
- ¾ oz. Coco López Cream of Coconut
- ½ oz. Falernum
- ½ oz. fresh lime juice
- 2 dashes Angostura bitters

1. Combine all of the ingredients, except for the bitters, in a cocktail shaker without ice and dry-shake.
2. Fill a pineapple glass with ice.
3. Pour the cocktail into the glass. Top with the bitters.
4. Garnish with an orange slice and a mint sprig and serve with a straw.

BARTENDER FOR HIRE

RED OWL TAVERN
433 CHESTNUT STREET

As the story goes, pharmacist Charles Hires brought his proprietary medicinal extract to the 1876 U.S. Centennial Exhibition in Philadelphia, introducing "Hires Root Beer" to the world. The drink was a childhood favorite of Red Owl Tavern's lead bartender Christopher Devern, who created the bourbon-based Bartender for Hire to mimic the soda's unmistakable vanilla, molasses and sassafras notes. A root beer reduction is used to bring down the overall carbonation and increase the overall flavor profile.

GLASSWARE: Coupe glass
GARNISH: Peychaud's bitters swirl, lemon twist

- 1 egg white
- ¾ oz. fresh lemon juice
- ¼ oz. Giffard Vanille de Madagascar
- ¾ oz. Root Beer Reduction (see recipe)
- 1⅕ oz. bourbon

1. Crack one egg white into a cocktail shaker tin, followed by fresh lemon juice and vanilla liqueur.
2. Add the root beer reduction and bourbon and dry-shake (without ice) vigorously for 15 seconds.
3. Add ice and shake again until the shaker tin is ice cold and condensation appears, about 20 seconds.

4. Double-strain the cocktail into a coupe, and serve up (cold but without ice).
5. Garnish with a lemon twist and Peychaud's bitters, swirled through with a toothpick.

ROOT BEER REDUCTION: In a saucepan over low heat, bring 1 (12 oz.) bottle of root beer to a low simmer for 10 minutes. Stir in 1 cup dark brown sugar until dissolved and turn off the heat. Let the mixture cool.

GARDEN SMASH

RED OWL TAVERN
433 CHESTNUT STREET

This easy-to-recreate Margarita celebrates the bounty of a summer garden. The star of the glass is a strawberry-infused tequila that's blended with Aperol for an eye-catching pop of pink. A basil agave syrup lends an aromatic and herbaceous backbone.

GLASSWARE: Stemless wineglass
GARNISH: Fresh basil leaves, strawberry slices

- 2 oz. Strawberry Infused Tequila-and-Aperol Blend (see recipe)
- ¾ oz. Basil Agave Syrup (see recipe)
- ¾ oz. fresh lime juice

1. Combine all of the ingredients in a cocktail shaker with ice.
2. Shake vigorously until well chilled, about 10 seconds.
3. Strain the cocktail into a stemless wineglass with fresh ice. Garnish with fresh basil leaves and strawberry slices.

STRAWBERRY INFUSED TEQUILA-AND-APEROL BLEND: Slice 12 strawberries into thin pieces then add them to a container with 1 (750 ml) bottle of tequila and 8 oz. Aperol. Let the infusion sit for 5 to 7 days. You'll know the infusion is ready when the strawberries lose their red color and look white. Strain.

BASIL AGAVE SYRUP: In a saucepan over medium-high, bring ½ quart water to a boil. Add 20 sprigs of fresh basil, lower the heat, and simmer for 10 minutes. Add 1 quart agave nectar and stir until viscous. Allow the syrup to cool then strain.

MIDSUMMER NIGHT

STRATUS ROOFTOP LOUNGE
433 CHESTNUT STREET

True to its name, this crushable and fruity vodka cocktail evokes the energy of warm summer nights overlooking the streets of Philadelphia. The flavor is reminiscent of a pink Starburst candy. This popular order is low-stress, approachable, and most importantly, delicious.

GLASSWARE: Martini glass
GARNISH: Fresh basil leaves, strawberry

- 1½ oz. Cucumber Vodka (see recipe)
- ½ oz. Licor 43
- ¾ oz. Strawberry Syrup (see recipe)
- ½ oz. fresh lime juice

1. Combine all of the ingredients in a cocktail shaker with ice and shake.
2. Strain the cocktail into a martini glass. Garnish with fresh basil leaves and a strawberry on the rim.

CUCUMBER VODKA: Peel and slice 1 whole cucumber into ½-inch disks, then add the pieces to 1 (750 ml) bottle of vodka. Store the cucumber infusion in the refrigerator for 2 days. Strain.

STRAWBERRY SYRUP: Hull and dice 1 pint strawberries into quarters, then combine the strawberries in a blender with 1 cup boiling water and 1 cup granulated white sugar. Blend on high until the consistency becomes a viscous liquid. Strain the syrup through a fine-mesh strainer into a fresh container and let the syrup settle for about 1 hour.

SHAWN MILLER, FORSYTHIA

How did you get your start bartending?

I got my start in this industry from just a high school job dishwashing and working the counter at a deli. I didn't realize this would become a career. I became a server, and then eventually went to culinary school for pastry and discovered that the skills and creativity I learned there could also be applied to the bar.

What do you enjoy most about bartending?

What I must enjoy about bartending is expressing myself creatively through the drinks, and as a lover of history, as someone who enjoys learning about wine. And the fact that I don't have to sit at a desk—I get to interact with people for a living—is amazing.

What is unique about Forsythia's bar program?

The bar program at Forsythia is unique in that we try to mirror our savory menu, folding in as many local and seasonal ingredients into drinks. We refer to it as a farm-to-glass approach. The wine, to match our cuisine, is almost exclusively French. We try to represent as many regions and styles of French wine as possible.

What are the top two or three things home bartenders can do to up their game?

The home bartender can definitely up their game by trying to create their own syrups, tinctures, cordials, and bitters whenever possible. If you are already using store-bought products or using flavored spirits, try to replicate those flavors on your own at home. Shrubs are a great way to start, because they provide fruit and acid and can store for quite a long time.

In a few sentences, how would you characterize the cocktail community in Philadelphia?

The beverage scene in Philadelphia is very vibrant. Because it's been kind of considered an underdog and more affordable major city for a long time, people were able to think outside the box. There is also a huge diversity of cultures represented in the restaurant scene and a lot of them try to represent their distinct regional flavors in their cocktails.

CARROT ME HOME

FORSYTHIA
233 CHESTNUT STREET

Forsythia prides itself on its use of seasonal ingredients. In the fall and winter months, beverage director Shawn Miller gravitates toward root vegetables in cocktails, especially carrot, as they add subtle sweetness and earthiness. He is also a fan of using vinegars in drinks, usually in the form of shrubs or gastriques, as a way of adding acidity without always relying citrus. The gastrique in this recipe creates a unique and addictive vegetal sweet-and-sour flavor. The amaro adds eucalyptus and cinnamon that play well with the baking spice of the bourbon.

GLASSWARE: Rocks glass
GARNISH: Lemon twist, edible flowers

- 1¾ oz. bourbon
- 1 oz. Carrot Gastrique (see recipe)
- ¼ oz. fresh lemon juice
- 2 barspoons Forthave Spirits MARSEILLE Amaro
- 2 dashes orange bitters
- 2 dashes ginger bitters

1. Combine all of the ingredients in a cocktail shaker with ice and shake.
2. Strain the cocktail into a rocks glass.
3. Top with ice and garnish with a lemon twist and edible flowers.

Carrot Gastrique: In a blender, puree 2 quarts chopped carrots, 1 quart apple cider vinegar, and the juice of one large orange. Meanwhile, in a large saucepot over medium heat, combine 1 quart white sugar and 1 cup water and simmer, until the mixture turns a straw yellow (don't stir), about 20 minutes. Add the carrot puree and 3 teaspoons loose-leaf turmeric-ginger tea to the pot and stir vigorously. Let mixture come back to a simmer for 5 minutes. Strain.

ISLAY ROSES ON YOUR GRAVE

FORSYTHIA
233 CHESTNUT STREET

Robust peated scotch, while excellent on its own, can quickly overpower a cocktail. In this cleverly named drink, Forsythia beverage director Shawn Miller complements the spirit's smoky and salty notes with floral and herbaceous liqueurs and a zip of citrus.

GLASSWARE: Coupe glass
GARNISH: Edible flower

- ¾ oz. Laphroaig Oak Select
- ¾ oz. Dolin Génépy le Chamois Liqueur
- ¾ oz. Combier Liqueur de Rose
- ½ oz. fresh lemon juice
- ¼ oz. grapefruit juice

1. Combine all of the ingredients in a cocktail tin.
2. Fill with ice and shake vigorously until chilled and combined, about 15 seconds.
3. Double-strain the cocktail into a coupe glass. Garnish with an edible flower.

PIÑA COLOBSTA

FORSYTHIA
233 CHESTNUT STREET

Forsythia's cocktails often take cues from the kitchen's French cooking. This imaginative crustacean-inspired milk punch was created to accompany a lobster dinner. It gets a richness from lobster butter–washed rum and beachy notes from pineapple and coconut. Beverage director Shawn Miller describes it as a "softer, sophisticated, and more subtle tropical drink." The recipe is designed for batching, making it ideal for entertaining.

GLASSWARE: Coupe glass
GARNISH: Lime twist

- 33 oz. Fat-Washed Rum Blend (see recipe)
- 16½ oz. coconut water
- 11 oz. Simple Syrup (see recipe on page 11)
- 12½ oz. pineapple juice
- 10 oz. Spiced Cognac (see recipe)
- 9½ oz. fresh lime juice
- 9 oz. whole milk

1. Mix all of the ingredients together in a large container and then add the milk last.
2. Allow the mixture to curdle and sit for 20 minutes. Strain it through a colander with a coffee filter laid inside. (The coffee filter may need to be changed out a few times).

3. Bottle and refrigerate the punch.
4. Serve 3 oz. of the chilled cocktail in a coupe and garnish with a lime twist.

Fat-Washed Rum Blend: In a large container, combine 20½ oz. Planteray 5 Years Rum, 12½ oz. white rum, and 2½ oz. melted lobster compound butter. Let the mixture sit out for at least 4 hours, then freeze it overnight. Strain out and discard the solids.

Spiced Cognac: In a glass container, combine 1 (750 ml) bottle of cognac with 10 whole cloves; 1 small piece of ginger, peeled and sliced; and the zest of 1 lime. Let the mixture sit overnight then strain and stir.

LES PAUL

48 RECORD BAR
48 SOUTH 2ND STREET

This riff on a fifty-fifty perfect Gin Gibson gets a name that will make musicians smile. The recipe traces itself back to a 1960s-themed party. According to bartender Lauren Levin, the chef found himself with surplus of brine for his pickled red onions, and the bar had separately been workshopping a recipe for celery bitters. A dash of MSG ties together the salty-sweet-vegetal notes into a smooth and drinkable cocktail, even for those who prefer their martinis clean. And, she says, don't forget the parsley oil drop garnish—it brings a psychedelic, 1960s aesthetic and a surprising amount of complementary flavor and aroma.

GLASSWARE: Nick & Nora glass
GARNISH: Parsley Oil (see recipe)

- 1½ oz. Plymouth Gin
- ¾ oz. Lo-Fi Aperitifs Dry Vermouth
- ½ oz. Red Onion Brine (see recipe)
- ¾ oz. Lo-Fi Aperitifs Sweet Vermouth
- 6 dashes celery bitters
- ½ barspoon MSG

1. Chill a Nick & Nora glass. Combine all of the ingredients in a stirring glass with ice and stir until well chilled.
2. Strain the cocktail into the chilled Nick & Nora.
3. Add three separate Parsley Oil droplets on the surface of the drink.

from 1 bunch of fresh parsley and flash boil for 45 seconds. Strain and run the parsley under cold water. Pat the parsley dry, add it to a blender with 1 cup olive oil, and blend. Strain the oil through a fine-mesh sieve or coffee filter. Store in a dropper bottle.

RED ONION BRINE: In a container, combine 1 cup water, 1 cup white vinegar, ¼ cup white sugar, and 1 oz. kosher salt and whisk until the salt and sugar are dissolved. Chop 3 red onions and submerge them in the mixture for 2 days. Strain.

LUCKY NUMBER

48 RECORD BAR
48 SOUTH 2ND STREET

When 48 Record Bar developed its second menu, the plan was to limit the drink list to an even dozen. But this take on a Midori Sour proved too deserving to be left out, so the bar team anointed it the lucky thirteenth cocktail. The recipe leans into the green color scheme, using some of the abundant cold-pressed cucumber juice from sister restaurant Sassafras along with mint bitters and a spritz of Green Chartreuse.

GLASSWARE: Nick & Nora glass
GARNISH: Dehydrated lemon wheel, Green Chartreuse spritz

- 2 oz. citrus vodka
- 1 oz. fresh lemon juice
- ¾ oz. Midori
- ½ oz. cucumber juice
- Dash mint bitters
- 1 egg white

1. Chill a Nick & Nora glass. Combine all of the ingredients in a cocktail shaker with one chip of ice and whip-shake until the chip dissolves.
2. Add more ice and shake briefly to chill the tin.
3. Fine-strain the cocktail into the chilled Nick & Nora.
4. Garnish with a dehydrated lemon wheel and a spritz of Green Chartreuse over the glass.

NEIL LAUGHLIN, SASSAFRAS

Neil Laughlin is a co-owner of Sassafras.

How did you get started in the bartending industry? And in Philadelphia specifically?

Thirty years ago, I landed in America with a couple hundred bucks in my pocket and a whole lot of hope. I was pounding the pavement, looking for work in Philadelphia, when I stopped into an Irish bar for lunch. I met an Irish guy named Tony O'Hare behind the bar while going to flight school, and he offered me a position barbacking. That began my journey.

What do you enjoy most about bartending?

Meeting the very broad range of people that come in, from attorneys to tattoo artists. It's understanding that people all have the same life struggles, just different viewpoints. It's great to introduce individuals from different walks of life to each other and get them in conversations they're not used to having.

What do you enjoy most about the Philadelphia cocktail community?

One of the great things about the Philadelphia cocktail community is the people that are doing it. Industry people have as much diversity in their background as the varied clientele that they serve. There are always great conversations, new skills to learn, and new tricks to be had.

STRAWBERRY STREET

SASSAFRAS
48 SOUTH 2ND STREET

Lead bartender Matt Hubsher and the team at Sassafras often introduce adventurous guests to off-menu syrups, juices, and bitters. These special ingredients turned into weekly specials, typically incorporated into an easily recognizable riff on a classic. Bourbon and Fernet give depth and sharpness to this strawberry rhubarb drink, named after a side street in Philadelphia's Old City neighborhood.

GLASSWARE: Lowball glass
GARNISH: Strawberry half, basil sprig

- 1½ oz. Buffalo Trace Bourbon
- 1 oz. Strawberry Puree (see recipe)
- 1 oz. Rhubarb Syrup (see recipe)
- ½ oz. fresh lemon juice
- ½ oz. Fernet-Branca
- Fistful of basil

1. Combine all of the ingredients in a cocktail shaker with ice and shake vigorously to ensure the basil is properly bruised.
2. Fine-strain the cocktail into a lowball glass over ice.
3. Garnish with a fresh basil sprig and a strawberry half.

STRAWBERRY PUREE: Nip the leafy ends off 1 pound strawberries, cut them in half, and then add them to a blender with ½ cup sugar and ½ cup water and blend. Push the puree through a fine-mesh sieve with a rubber spatula. Keep chilled for up to 2 weeks.

RHUBARB SYRUP: Trim the root and leafy ends off the stalks of 1 pound rhubarb. Chop the stalks into small slices no wider than 1 inch. In a pot over medium-high heat, combine the rhubarb with 1 cup water, 1 cup sugar, and 1 gram malic acid. Stir occasionally and adjust the heat to avoid a full rolling boil. Cook until the rhubarb has mostly dissolved, and then push the syrup through a fine-mesh sieve with a rubber spatula.

THE BOOG

THE TWISTED TAIL
509 SOUTH 2ND STREET

This bourbon cocktail is named after a The Twisted Tail regular, Gregg "The Boog" Williams. Gregg handpicks the blueberries for this cocktail in New Jersey and delivers them to The Twisted Tail. A quick honey simple syrup adds depth and sweetness that accents the unmistakable aroma of fresh rosemary.

GLASSWARE: Rocks glass
GARNISH: Blueberries, rosemary sprig

- **10 blueberries**
- **Sprig of rosemary**
- **2 lemon wedges**
- **½ oz. Honey Syrup (see recipe on page 167)**
- **1½ oz. Maker's Mark**

1. In a cocktail shaker, muddle 10 blueberries, 1 sprig of rosemary (leaves detached from the stem), and the 2 lemon wedges.
2. Add ice, Honey Syrup, and bourbon, and shake vigorously.
3. Strain the cocktail into a rocks glass over crushed ice and garnish with blueberries and a sprig of rosemary.

ROCKET FUEL

FORK
306 MARKET STREET

Created by bartender Matt Nelms, the Rocket Fuel is a take on the Jet Pilot, a timeless tiki cocktail. A trio of rums get stirred together along with other ingredients for a velvety clean mouthfeel.

GLASSWARE: Rocks glass
GARNISH: Dehydrated lime wheel

- 1 oz. Tenango Rum
- ½ oz. grapefruit liqueur
- ½ oz. Braulio Amaro
- ½ oz. Lime Cordial (see recipe)
- ¼ oz. Uruapan Charanda Blanco Rum
- ¼ oz. Lemon Hart 151 Demerara Rum
- ¼ oz. Cinnamon-Infused Rye Whiskey (see recipe)
- 4 drops Saline Solution (see recipe on page 11)

1. Combine all of the ingredients in a mixing glass with ice and stir well.
2. Strain the cocktail into a rocks glass with one large ice cube and garnish with a dehydrated lime wheel.

LIME CORDIAL: In a blender, combine 250 ml water, 250 grams cane sugar, 1 oz. fresh lime juice, and 4/5 oz. citric acid and blend thoroughly.

CINNAMON-INFUSED RYE WHISKEY: In a bottle or other container, combine 4 to 5 cinnamon sticks and 500 ml rye whiskey. Allow the infusion to sit for at least 24 hours at room temperature.

SCORCHED ATLAS

FORK
306 MARKET STREET

Scorched Atlas is credited to the Fork bartender pair of Rodney Murray and Matt Nelms. The cocktail is built to be a nuanced take on the Rob Roy (essentially a scotch Manhattan).

GLASSWARE: Rocks glass
GARNISH: Lemon coin

- ¾ oz. Ardbeg Ten Years Old
- ¾ oz. Lustau Fino Jarana
- ¾ oz. Fell to Earth Sweet Vermouth
- ½ oz. Bonal Gentiane-Quina
- ¼ oz. Amaro Nonino Quintessentia
- 2 drops Saline Solution (see recipe on page 11)

1. Combine all of the ingredients in a mixing tin filled with ice and stir well.
2. Strain the cocktail into a rocks glass with a large rock and a lemon coin garnish.

LEMONANA

ZAHAV
237 ST. JAMES PLACE

Lemonana is a popular drink in Israel, often sold frozen by street vendors. The word is a combination of *limon* ("lemon" in Hebrew and *nana* ("mint"). It is the ubiquitous thirst quencher of Israel. Zahav introduces bourbon into the recipe for a cocktail that has become the restaurant's undisputed house favorite. The Lemonana evokes the spirit of a classic Whiskey Smash—and it's perfect for enjoying around a fire in service of cooking.

GLASSWARE: Rocks glass
GARNISH: Mint sprig

- 10 mint sprigs
- 1¼ oz. bourbon
- 1¼ oz. fresh lemon juice
- 1¼ oz. Lemon-Verbena-Mint Oleo Saccharum (see recipe)

1. In a cocktail shaker, muddle the mint sprigs with the bourbon.
2. Add the remaining ingredients and ice and shake well.
3. Strain the cocktail over ice and garnish with a mint sprig.

LEMON-VERBENA-MINT OLEO SACCHARUM: In an airtight container, combine 1 cup Sugar in the Raw, the peels of 6 lemons, ½ cup fresh mint leaves, and ¼ cup fresh verbena leaves, mix, and let sit for 24 hours to macerate. Add 1¼ cups warm water and stir to dissolve the remaining sugar. Strain the syrup to remove the herbs and lemon peels.

LIMONCELLO FRESCO SPRITZ

PANORAMA WINE BAR
14 NORTH FRONT STREET

Limoncello is a staple liqueur throughout Southern Italy and has its own proprietary recipe from one family to another. The Sena family is no exception. Originally from Naples, the Senas opened Penn's View Hotel and Panorama Wine Bar more than thirty years ago. Their family limoncello recipe remains highly protected, but any bottle will do to approximate this bright and refreshing cocktail at home.

GLASSWARE: Wineglass
GARNISH: Lemon wheel, baby basil sprig

- ½ oz. limoncello
- ½ oz. elderflower liqueur
- 3 oz. prosecco
- 1 oz. club soda, to top

1. Pour the limoncello over ice into a large wineglass.
2. Add the elderflower liqueur.
3. Add the prosecco and top with 1 oz club soda.
4. Float one sliced lemon wheel, topped with a sprig of baby basil, to garnish.

SOUTH STREET / QUEEN VILLAGE / SOUTH PHILLY

In the Body of Swan

The Special

Cider Gin Fizz

Solera Legacy

Fiori di Sicilia

Fall Seasonal Old Fashioned

Golden Revolver

Ladies Love Gin & Tonic

Good, Giving & Game

Prickly Pear Wasabi Mule

Tamale Old Fashioned

Negroni

Apple Brandy Sidecar

Espresso Martini

Dirty Pasta Water Martini

South Philly is best known for its famous dueling cheesesteaks, the vendors of the 9th Street Italian Market, and the shops and businesses of East Passyunk Avenue. Its neighborhood streets are densely lined with row houses and dotted with pocket parks, and bars—dive, upscale, and modern bistro-style—cater to hungry and thirsty locals all nights of the week. Make sure to visit Bob & Barbara's Lounge, a quintessential PA dive bar and the birthplace of Philadelphia's now-ubiquitous Citywide Special.

IN THE BODY OF SWAN

SOUTHWARK
701 SOUTH 4TH STREET

This three-ingredient recipe was created by Sterling Melcher and Randall Greenleaf, who wanted to create a cocktail that firmly represents Southwark. The apple brandy represents American heritage, Averna Amaro speaks to Italian roots, and Bonal Gentiane-Quina reflects French discipline. Each component exemplifies what makes Southwark special while paying homage to the classic Negroni.

GLASSWARE: Coupe glass
GARNISH: Orange peel

- 1 oz. Laird's Straight Apple Brandy Bottled in Bond
- 1 oz. Amaro Averna
- 1 oz. Bonal Gentiane-Quina

1. Combine all of the ingredients in a mixing glass and fill with ice and tir until well chilled and properly diluted.
2. Strain the cocktail into a coupe.
3. Garnish with an orange peel and enjoy.

BOB & BARBARA'S LOUNGE

Bob & Barbara's Lounge came to life on Philadelphia's South Street in 1969. While it's very much not the place for a craft cocktail—liquor is poured from the handle-sized bottles lining the bar—it's one of the city's quintessential dive bars, attracting guests with its weekly entertainment, low-key vibe, and famed beer-and-a-shot "Special."

The bar takes its name from its first owner, Robert Porter, and his manager, Barbara Carter. The pair operated the bar until 1994, when the business was sold to its current owner, Jack Prince.

The bar's iconic Special was introduced in 1995 by music promoter and bartender Rick Dombrowolski, aka Rick D. The bargain combo of a 12 oz. can of Pabst Blue Ribbon and a shot of Jim Beam was a way to attract midweek business and encourage guests to show up for the new slate of live music bookings. The Special was first sold for $3, or as little as $2.50 during happy hour. It remains a deal thirty years later, with the price having increased only to $5.

Looking around the bar, it's clear that the Special caught on. The walls and ceilings are peppered with Pabst and Jim Beam memorabilia, from lamps and mirrors to signs and vintage advertisements.

The Special caught on at other Philadelphia bars so much that it was nicknamed "The Citywide." Variations of the beer-and-a-shot favorite are seen at bars around the city (and even regionally), with some sticking to the classic pairing while others set out to match different beers and spirits together. Though as Jack Prince says, Bob & Barbara's deal is "often imitated, never duplicated."

Aside from beer and liquor, Bob and Barbara's is a destination for a wide range of events, including the longest running drag show in the country. There's also karaoke, live bands, jam sessions, and DJ nights. The centerpiece of the stage is a rare Hammond B3 organ bequeathed to the bar in 2006 in the will of Philadelphia musician Nate Wiley, of famed group Nate Wiley & the Crowd Pleasers.

Today, Bob and Barbara's is run by Prince's stepchildren, Katrina and Oskar. The brother-and-sister pair are staying true to the DNA of the bar, including pouring many a $5 Special while continuing to add new programming that will bring both regulars and new guests through the doors. And if you're lucky, they might switch on the disco ball that hangs above the bar while you enjoy a round or two.

THE SPECIAL

BOB & BARBARA'S LOUNGE
1509 SOUTH STREET

Regulars and visitors alike congregate at this cash-only dive bar for its famous five-dollar beer-and-a-shot Special. The price has increased just two dollars since it was first advertised in 1995 by current owner Jack Prince. The deal became so popular that it spread to bars across Philadelphia, giving rise to the "Citywide"—the local term for this classic combo.

GLASSWARE: Shot glass

- ¾ oz. Jim Beam
- 1 (12 oz.) can of Pabst Blue Ribbon

1. Open the can of beer.
2. Pour the bourbon into a shot glass.
3. Enjoy.

CIDER GIN FIZZ

HALE & TRUE CIDER CO.
613 SOUTH 7TH STREET

House-made cider takes the place of champagne in this riff on a French 75. The cocktail has been on the Hale & True menu since the cidery opened in 2018 and has become a bestseller. Owner Kerry McKenzie started Hale & True to showcase the possibilities of what cider could be, incorporating ingredients like honey, hops, and fruit with fresh-pressed, fermented cider. The Cider Gin Fizz proves the versatility of cider, highlighting the nuances of the apple, honey, and ginger notes and blending perfectly with Philadelphia-made gin.

GLASSWARE: Stemmed beer glass
GARNISH: Lemon peel

- 1½ oz. Bluecoat American Dry Gin
- ½ oz. Simple Syrup (see recipe on page 11)
- ½ oz. fresh lemon juice
- 2 oz. Hale & True Bee Sting Cider, to top

1. In a shaker, combine the gin, lemon juice, and simple syrup.
2. Add ice to the shaker, cover, and shake until well chilled.
3. Strain the cocktail into a stemmed beer glass filled with ice.
4. Top with cider and garnish with a lemon peel.

SOLERA LEGACY

IRWIN'S
800 MIFFLIN STREET

The Solera Legacy is Spain in a glass. Bartender Damián Langarica stirs together two types of sherry and blends them with a preserved lemon juice for a touch of citrusy sweetness. Its lack of a true spirit means it is lower in alcohol content than a typical cocktail, making it a good option for those days or nights when you want to take life at a slower pace.

GLASSWARE: Coupe glass
GARNISH: Orange twist, grated cinnamon

- ¾ oz. Spiced Demerara Syrup (see recipe)
- ½ oz. Preserved Lemon Juice (see recipe)
- 2 oz. Lustau Oloroso Don Nuño
- ½ oz. Lustau Pedro Ximénez San Emilio

1. Chill a coupe glass. Combine all of the ingredients, except for the Pedro Ximénez sherry, in a cocktail shaker with ice and shake.
2. Strain the cocktail into the chilled coupe.
3. Pour the Pedro Ximénez sherry down a barspoon to the bottom of the coupe to create a layering effect.
4. Garnish with an orange twist and grated cinnamon.

SPICED DEMERARA SYRUP: In a pot over medium heat, combine 500 grams Sugar in the Raw, 250 grams water, 15 grams cardamon, ½ whole nutmeg, grated, 15 grams cloves, 15 grams allspice, and 7 cinnamon sticks and stir until the sugar dissolves. Allow the syrup to cool, strain, and store it in the refrigerator until ready to use.

PRESERVED LEMON JUICE: Juice 3 lemons and reserve the juice. In a container, use the spent citrus rinds to make oleo with equal parts salt and sugar by weight. In a separate container, combine 3⅓ oz. (100 ml) lemon juice with ½ oz. (15 ml) lemon oleo.

FIORI DI SICILIA

IRWIN'S
800 MIFFLIN STREET

This drink is subtly nutty and savory thanks to its key ingredient—a toasted almond-infused bianco vermouth. The base spirit is grappa, an Italian grape spirit.

GLASSWARE: Nick & Nora glass
GARNISH: Spritz of Fiori di Sicilia Extract

- 1¼ oz. Grappa Nardini
- ½ oz. Luxardo Bitter Bianco
- ¼ oz. Salers Gentian Apéritif
- 1 oz. Toasted Almond-Infused Bianco Vermouth (see recipe)

1. Chill a Nick & Nora glass. Combine all of the ingredients in a mixing glass with ice.
2. Stir until the drink is properly chilled, then strain it into the chilled Nick & Nora.
3. Garnish with a spritz of Fiori di Sicilia Extract.

TOASTED ALMOND–INFUSED BIANCO VERMOUTH: Toast 75 grams shriveled almonds in an oven until golden brown. Combine the toasted almonds with 500 ml bianco vermouth and leave it to infuse overnight. Strain.

FALL SEASONAL OLD FASHIONED

THE PUB ON PASSYUNK EAST
1501 EAST PASSYUNK AVENUE

Greet the crisp air and fall holidays with this Old Fashioned twist from bartender Kevin Walsh. It gets its warming notes from a bourbon infused with chai tea spices, along with a zippy sweetness from honey ginger syrup. Walsh says the idea came from a previous stint working in a brunch restaurant where they served a fantastic house-made chai.

GLASSWARE: Rocks glass
GARNISH: Orange twist

- 2 oz. Chai Tea–Infused Bourbon (see recipe)
- ½ oz. honey ginger syrup
- 2 dashes Angostura bitters
- 2 dashes Regans' Orange Bitters No. 6

1. Combine all of the ingredients in a mixing glass with ice and stir.
2. Strain the cocktail into a rocks glass and garnish with an orange twist.

CHAI TEA–INFUSED BOURBON: Add 3 to 4 bags of chai tea to 1 (750 ml) bottle of bourbon. Let it steep for 12 hours. Remove the tea bags before serving.

GOLDEN REVOLVER

SOUTH PHILADELPHIA TAP ROOM
1509 MIFFLIN STREET

Don't be distracted by the tap room name: this bourbon-powered espresso-based cocktail is sure to become a customer favorite at this neighborhood pub. It features a fantastic Pennsylvania-made craft coffee liqueur and Averna, one of the staff's favorite amari. Think of it like an Espresso Manhattan of sorts. The technique of a dry shake (shaking without adding ice) creates a nice frothy top layer. If you can't source espresso, you can use double-strength cold brew coffee.

GLASSWARE: Coupe glass
GARNISH: Coffee beans

- 1 oz. espresso
- 1½ oz. Maggie's Farm Coffee Liqueur
- 1 oz. Medley Bros. Kentucky Straight Bourbon Whiskey
- ½ oz. Simple Syrup (see recipe on page 11)
- ¼ oz. Amaro Averna

1. Combine all of the ingredients in a cocktail shaker without ice and dry-shake for 30 seconds.
2. Add ice and shake again.
3. Strain the cocktail into a coupe and garnish with 3 coffee beans.

LADIES LOVE GIN & TONIC

SOUTH PHILADELPHIA TAP ROOM
1509 MIFFLIN STREET

A syrup made from butterfly pea flower gives a vibrant purple hue to this Gin and Tonic variation. Flavors of lavender and lemon blend harmoniously with the American dry gin to make this fun and refreshing Philly take on the British classic.

GLASSWARE: Highball glass
GARNISH: Lemon wheel

- 1½ oz. Bluecoat American Dry Gin
- ½ oz. Lavender Syrup (see recipe)
- ½ oz. fresh lemon juice
- 4 oz. Fever-Tree Premium Indian Tonic Water

1. Combine all of the ingredients, except for the tonic water, in a cocktail shaker filled with ice.
2. Shake well, about 10 seconds.
3. Strain the cocktail into a highball glass filled with fresh ice.
4. Top with tonic water and garnish with a lemon wheel.

LAVENDER SYRUP: Combine 125 grams boiling water, 125 grams sugar, 2 grams butterfly pea flower, and 1 gram dried lavender flowers in a pot or other heat-safe container. Stir to dissolve the sugar and let the mixture steep for 30 minutes. Strain the syrup through a fine-mesh strainer and chill it.

GOOD, GIVING & GAME

GRACE & PROPER
941 SOUTH 8TH STREET

The Good, Giving & Game is a Grace & Proper house favorite, holding a spot on the menu since the restaurant opened in November 2022. General Manager Ryan Rayer says it's based on the classic Bee's Knees and is testament to the virtue of keeping things simple and an homage to the innovation of bar craftsmen throughout the years. This graceful cocktail uses gin infused with saffron, the world's most expensive spice, and is adorned with real 24-karat gold flakes. The name comes from Dan Savage's Sex-Advice Column "Savage Love," where Good, Giving & Game, or "GGG", are the qualities he advises you to seek in a lover.

GLASSWARE: Coupe glass
GARNISH: Edible 24K gold flakes

- 2 oz. Saffron-Infused Gin (see recipe)
- ¾ oz. Honey Syrup (see recipe)
- ¾ oz. fresh lime juice
- 1 grapefruit peel

1. Chill a coupe glass. Combine all of the ingredients in a shaker tin with ice and firmly shake until the tin gets frosty, about 15 seconds.
2. Fine-strain the cocktail into the chilled coupe.
3. Garnish with edible 24-karat gold flakes.

HONEY SYRUP: In a pot or saucepan, combine 9 oz. honey and 3 oz. boiling water (3:1 ratio). Stir until the honey is dissolved.

SAFFRON-INFUSED GIN: Add 170 milligrams saffron to 1 (750 ml) bottle of gin and gently shake. Let the bottle sit for 3 hours, gently shaking occasionally. Strain and rebottle.

PRICKLY PEAR WASABI MULE

AMERICAN SARDINE BAR
1800 FEDERAL STREET

Bartender Meghan O'Connor has a voracious appetite when it comes to examining interethnic relationships. When she's not physically traipsing around the globe, she explores these cultures through her connections at home in Philadelphia—often through food and drink. One such friendship piqued an interest in Japanese emigration to Mexico and the rise of the Little Tokyo neighborhood in Mexico City.

GLASSWARE: Rocks or mule glass
GARNISH: Lime wheel

- 2 oz. Condesa Gin Clásica
- ½ oz. Wasabi Syrup (see recipe)
- ¾ oz. cactus pear puree
- ½ oz. fresh lemon juice
- Ginger beer, to top

1. Build all of the ingredients over ice in a large rocks glass or mule glass.
2. Garnish with a lime wheel.

WASABI SYRUP: In a saucepan over medium heat, bring 2 cups water to a boil. Add 200 grams granulated sugar and 1½ tablespoons wasabi powder, lower the heat to a simmer, and stir until the sugar is dissolved. Allow the syrup to cool.

TAMALE OLD FASHIONED

AMERICAN SARDINE BAR
1800 FEDERAL STREET

General manager Bonnie Garbinski developed this drink after her first trip to Oaxaca, wanting to capture the spirit of the place and its people. Good-quality mezcal and mole bitters help to bring the vibrant energy of Mexico to Philadelphia's Point Breeze neighborhood. If Agave de Cortés is unavailable, Garbinski suggests looking for a joven espadin mezcal with notes of honey, tropical fruit, and pepper. Nuestra Soledad and Rey Campero Espadin are two good options. An overly smoky mezcal, she says, will overpower the subtle flavors of the other ingredients.

GLASSWARE: Rocks glass
GARNISH: Orange peel, expressed

- 2 oz. Agave de Cortés Joven Mezcal
- ½ oz. Giffard Banane du Brésil
- 6 drops Bittermens Xocolatl Mole Bitters

1. Combine all of the ingredients in a rocks glass.
2. Add a little ice, express the orange peel over the drink, and add the peel as a garnish.
3. Stir for 20 to 30 seconds.

NEGRONI

MANATAWNY STILL WORKS
VARIOUS LOCATIONS

Manatawny Still Works makes its negroni with its namesake oak barrel–rested gin. The gin spends several months in ex-whiskey barrels, which brings on flavors like vanilla, caramel, and spice. The resulting Negroni is reminiscent of the classic Boulevardier. Due to regulations placed on Pennsylvania distilleries, Manatawny does not have access to imported spirits like Campari, so they instead use an aperitivo from local company Boardroom Spirits and a sweet vermouth made by Fell to Earth.

GLASSWARE: Rocks glass
GARNISH: Orange twist, expressed

- 1 oz. Manatawny Still Works Gin Finished in Oak Barrels
- 1 oz. Fell to Earth Sweet Vermouth
- 1 oz. Boardroom Spirits The Chairman's Aperitivo

1. Build all of the ingredients in a rocks glass over a big rock of ice.
2. Stir until chilled, about 10 seconds.
3. Garnish with an expressed orange twist.

APPLE BRANDY SIDECAR

MANATAWNY STILL WORKS
VARIOUS LOCATIONS

Manatawny makes its Sidecar with its own apple brandy, distilled from a cider made with seventeen varieties of apples grown at Big Hill Ciderworks in Adams County, Pennsylvania. The spirit is bright and bracing with a strong apple note on the nose. This classic twentieth-century cocktail uses the aromas of fruits to trick the senses into disregarding the considerable amount of alcohol within. The finish on this is on the drier side, allowing the spirits to shine. The tartness of the drink is well balanced by the sugared rim.

GLASSWARE: Coupe

- Cinnamon, for the rim
- Demerara sugar, for the rim
- 2 oz. Manatawny Still Works Apple Brandy
- ½ oz. orange liqueur
- 1 oz. fresh lemon juice
- ½ oz. Simple Syrup (see recipe on page 11)
- Orange peel, expressed

1. Chill a coupe glass. Wet the rim of the chilled coupe with an orange peel, then dip the glass in a mix of cinnamon and demerara sugar to give the glass a rim.
2. Combine the remaining ingredients, except for the orange peel, in a cocktail shaker filled with ice.
3. Shake until well chilled, about 10 seconds.
4. Strain the cocktail into the chilled and rimmed coupe.
5. Express an orange twist over the cocktail then discard the peel.

ESPRESSO MARTINI

MANATAWNY STILL WORKS
VARIOUS LOCATIONS

Since Pennsylvania's liquor laws require craft producers to use only Pennsylvania-made beer, wine, and spirits in its tasting rooms, the bar team at Manatawny often has to get creative. This different side of the Espresso Martini is spirit-forward and not for the faint of heart. It showcases the flavor combination of salt, chocolate, caramel, and coffee. The fun part is that it packs the punch of cask-strength whiskey in place of vodka. In fact, the tasting room cocktail menu explicitly dissuades customers from inquiring about the ingredients, asking instead for them to place trust in the bartender.

GLASSWARE: Nick & Nora glass

- Chocolate bitters–and–Saline Solution (see recipe on page 11) spritz
- 1 oz. cask-strength whiskey
- 1 oz. concentrated cold brew coffee
- 1 oz. coffee liqueur
- ½ oz. oleo saccharum

1. Freeze a Nick & Nora. Spritz the frozen glass with a blend of chocolate bitters and saline solution.
2. Combine the remaining ingredients in a cocktail shaker filled with ice.
3. Shake well, about 10 seconds.
4. Strain the cocktail into the chilled Nick & Nora.

DIRTY PASTA WATER MARTINI

FIORELLA
817 CHRISTIAN STREET

This Martini's reuse of salted cooked pasta water makes it an ideal accompaniment for a spaghetti dinner at home. It's also a go-to at Fiorella, chef Marc Vetri's casual South Philadelphia pasta spot. The drink shines with either gin or vodka, so feel free to choose whichever spirit is preferred—or on hand. The recipe is credited to Fiorella's opening bartender, Kyle Darrow, who now co-owns Fishtown's Next of Kin.

GLASSWARE: Nick & Nora glass
GARNISH: Skewer with 3 olives

- 2 oz. Boardroom Vodka
- ½ oz. salted pasta water
- ½ oz. olive brine

1. Combine all of the ingredients in a Boston shaker with ice.
2. Shake well until diluted and chilled.
3. Double-strain the cocktail into a Nick & Nora and garnish with 3 olives.

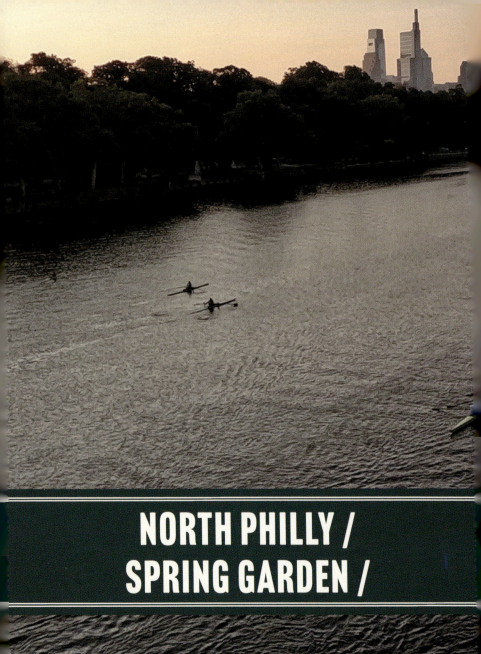

NORTH PHILLY / SPRING GARDEN /

NORTHERN LIBERTIES / FISHTOWN / SUBURBS

CLOVER CLUB	SOUL FASHIONED
PENSYLVANIA PUNCH	RIDIN' DIRTY
MUTTER'S CHARM	CELEBRITY SKIN
NO CALL, NO SHOW	BITCHIN' CAMARO
MOONJUICE	IT'S ALL GUAVA, BABY
VIETNAM BAR	OUR DAILY VEDGE
SMOKE & BARRELS	BLOOD, SWEAT AND CHEERS
TONIQUE	GETTIN' CHILI OUT
SEAWATER MARGARITA	BAY SIDE SNAP
PILKARZ	THAT'S FASHION BABY!
LOLLOVE VILLAGE	KASUGAI SOUR
BASTIA SPRITZ	SADŌTINI
GREEN LIGHT	THE WAR ON CHRISTMAS
SOULMONGER	HIGHWAY ROBBERY
THE PLEASURE CLUB OF FIUMEDINISI	UNTITLED
CLASSIC WHISKEY SOUR	

Head to the dense neighborhoods sprawling across North Philadelphia, from river to river, the Schuylkill in the west and the Delaware in the east, for an experience away from the tourists and crowds of Center City. Northern Liberties, or NoLibs as locals call it, where the Market-Frankford Line runs above the city streets, has earned its reputation for exciting nightlife, and the cocktail scene along North Broad Street is becoming more attractive by the year.

CLOVER CLUB

PHILADELPHIA DISTILLING
25 EAST ALLEN STREET

This fragrant Gin Sour variation was the house drink of The Clover Club, an organization that met in Philadelphia's Bellevue Stratford Hotel Bar from the early 1800s right up until the start of World War I. It's one of the few classic cocktails invented right here in Philadelphia, and there are few ways more appropriate to enjoy it than with Philadelphia Distilling's flagship gin.

GLASSWARE: Coupe glass
GARNISH: Raspberry on a skewer

- 2 oz. Bluecoat American Dry Gin
- 1 egg white
- ¾ oz. fresh lemon juice
- ¾ oz. Raspberry Syrup (see recipe)

1. Combine all of the ingredients in a cocktail shaker without ice and dry-shake for 30 seconds to emulsify the egg white.
2. Add ice and gently wet-shake.
3. Double-strain the cocktail into a coupe.
4. Garnish with a skewered raspberry.

Raspberry Syrup: In a large kitchen storage container, combine 225 grams fresh raspberries, 225 grams sugar, and 2 oz. Dolin Dry Vermouth. Using a ladle or a rolling pin, smash the ingredients together until the mixture becomes mostly liquid. Let the mixture macerate for 24 hours. Blend the mixture using an immersion blender, then fine-strain the syrup and bottle.

PENSYLVANIA PUNCH

PHILADELPHIA DISTILLING
25 EAST ALLEN STREET

The "Pensylvania" in the name of this citrus-forward gin punch is spelled with one "n," and it's no accident. It's a nod to American history, as the state's name was spelled with only one "n" both on the Liberty Bell and in the Constitution. The team at Philadelphia Distilling originally crafted this gin punch as a sustainability project for the bar, using whatever leftover fruit juice remained from the citrus used to garnish cocktails throughout the week.

GLASSWARE: Wineglass
GARNISH: Orange slice

- 1½ oz. Bluecoat American Dry Gin
- 1½ oz. orange juice
- ½ oz. Honey Syrup (see recipe on page 11)
- ½ oz. fresh lemon juice
- ¼ oz. Aperol
- Splash club soda, to top

1. Combine all of the ingredients, except for the soda, in a wineglass, add ice, and stir.
2. Top with club soda and garnish with an orange slice.

MUTTER'S CHARM

PHILADELPHIA DISTILLING
25 EAST ALLEN STREET

Bartender Canyon Shayer features four ingredients in equal parts to arrive at this approachable absinthe cocktail. The drink is essentially a variation of the Corpse Reviver, hence the fitting name in honor of Philadelphia's Mutter Museum and its fascination with the curiosities of the human body.

GLASSWARE: Coupe glass
GARNISH: Lemon twist, expressed

- ¾ oz. Vieux Carré Absinthe Supérieure
- ¾ oz. fresh lemon juice
- ¾ oz. Honey Syrup (see recipe on page 11)
- ¾ oz. Aperol

1. Chill a coupe glass. Combine all of the ingredients in a cocktail tin filled with ice.
2. Shake well until chilled and combined, about 10 seconds.
3. Strain the cocktail into the chilled coupe and garnish with an expressed lemon twist.

NO CALL, NO SHOW

JAFFA BAR
1625 NORTH HOWARD STREET

This newly opened bar comes from the restaurant group behind Zahav. The renovated firehouse is an inspired backdrop for the menu of hot and cold dishes that focus on seafood and Mediterranean flavors. The No Call, No Show, says creator bartender Sean Byrne, is a modified Hanky Panky, traditionally a three-ingredient drink with gin, sweet vermouth, and Fernet-Branca.

GLASSWARE: Coupe glass
GARNISH: Lemon twist

- 1½ oz. Beefeater Gin
- ¾ oz. Fell to Earth Sweet Vermouth
- ½ oz. Amaro Meletti
- ½ oz. Fernet-Branca

1. Chill a coupe glass. Combine all of the ingredients in a mixing glass with ice.
2. Stir well until chilled, about 10 seconds.
3. Strain the cocktail into the chilled coupe and garnish with a lemon twist.

MOONJUICE

THE INTERNATIONAL BAR
1624 NORTH FRONT STREET

General manager Ceallaigh Corbishley leans on several local producers for The International Bar, including making Martinis with fresh olive brine. One day, Philadelphia's Perrystead Dairy challenged him to use the leftover whey from its Moonrise cheese. Instead of fat-washing, a common bartending technique when working with dairy, the whey in this cocktail goes straight into the shaker. Corbishley credits the creation to his bartender AJ and says the drink will be on the menu as long as there's access to fresh whey.

GLASSWARE: Coupe glass
GARNISH: Mint sprig, black lime ash

- 1½ oz. Principe De Los Apostoles Mate Gin
- ¾ oz. whey
- ½ oz. Vanilla Bean Simple Syrup (see recipe)
- ½ oz. fresh lemon juice
- 3 barspoons crème de violette
- 3 drops Saline Solution (see recipe)

1. Combine all of the ingredients in a cocktail shaker with ice.
2. Shake well until chilled and combined, about 15 seconds.
3. Strain the cocktail into a coupe and garnish with a mint sprig and black lime ash.

Vanilla Bean Simple Syrup: Split 3 vanilla beans open and cut the beans into thirds. In a saucepan, combine the beans, 16 oz. white sugar, and 16 oz. boiling water and stir to dissolve the sugar. Let the syrup sit for 5 minutes. Remove the beans.

Saline Solution: Combine 13 oz. boiling water and 3 oz. kosher salt in a container and stir until the salt is dissolved. Store the solution in a dropper bottle.

VIETNAM BAR

THE INTERNATIONAL BAR
1624 NORTH FRONT STREET

This cocktail is inspired by a barrel tasting trip that general manager Ceallaigh Corbishley and head bartender Jess Craine took to the Tromba tequila distillery in Jalisco, Mexcico. Their accommodation was next to a smoky dive bar in Guadalajara named "Vietnam bar," and the two spent most of their nights there, drawn to both the vibe and the extensive collection of agave spirits. You can use Green Chartreuse (if you can find it) in place of the Faccio Brutto.

GLASSWARE: Rocks glass

- 1½ oz. Granja Nómada Espadín
- ¾ oz. of Mint Simple Syrup (see recipe)
- ½ oz. fresh lime juice
- ½ oz. Centerbe Faccia Brutto
- 3 dashes Ghost Pepper Tincture (see recipe)

1. Combine all of the ingredients in a cocktail shaker with both large and crushed ice cubes.
2. Shake until chilled.
3. Strain the cocktail over fresh ice into a large rocks glass.

Mint Simple Syrup: Combine 8 oz. sugar, 10 grams mint, and 8 oz. boiling water in a container and stir until the sugar is dissolved. Let the syrup steep for 10 minutes. Remove the mint.

Ghost Pepper Tincture: In a large container or bottle, combine 2 ghost peppers and 1 (750 ml) bottle of Everclear and let the infusion sit overnight. Remove the peppers. Use with a dropper bottle.

KYLE DARROW, NEXT OF KIN

At Fishtown's Next of Kin, atmosphere and hospitality are just as important as what's in the glass. "We wanted to bring the cocktail world down to where Philly is as a city," says Kyle Darrow, one of the bar's three co-owners. "We wanted to be that neighborhood hangout."

Next of Kin is the culmination of many years of bartending experience for Darrow, who worked at Kimpton Hotels in Philadelphia. He was also the opening bar manager at Marc Vetri's Fiorella. Next of Kin's two other partners include Darrow's brother-in-law, Devan Roberts, and mutual friend John Grubb, himself an accomplished bartender around the city.

The energetic cocktail lounge delivers on approachability, with drinks grouped by flavor profile and base spirits. It's a menu that's easy to decipher and enjoy. The goal is to be fun, not complicated. "People can be in and out of the menu pretty quickly, without having to Google any weird ingredients," Darrow says.

That's not to take away from the craft of the team. Next of Kin serves up a wide range of cocktails, from classics to originals. And there's plenty of cocktail science going on behind the bar, with recipes that incorporate techniques like infusing and fat-washing. "We try to have fun with it, and we enjoy the creative part of it as well," Darrow says.

Next of Kin is also making a point to revive drinks that have gotten lost in the shuffle, such as the French Martini or the Corn 'n' Oil—a boozy tiki sipper with rum, falernum, lime, and Angostura bitters. The bar also keeps a running batch of index cards they use to keep track of one-off creations and customer favorites.

Devan Roberts (left), John Grubb (center), Kyle Darrow (right)

SMOKE & BARRELS

NEXT OF KIN
1414 FRANKFORD AVENUE

Smoke & Barrels is the first cocktail the Next of Kin team of Kyle Darrow, John Grubb, and Devan Roberts created when they started bartending together. The original ideal of a smoked Manhattan riff has evolved over the years to this deceptively smooth sipper that offers both simplicity and approachability. It's been featured on menus at multiple bars, and the team says they've lost count as to how many times they've written down this recipe for guests.

GLASSWARE: Martini glass
GARNISH: Cherry

- 1¾ oz. rye whiskey
- ¾ oz. mezcal
- ½ oz. amaro
- Barspoon cherry liquid

1. Chill a martini glass. Combine all of the ingredients in a mixing glass with ice and stir well, until chilled and combined.
2. Strain the cocktail into the chilled martini glass and garnish with a cherry.

TONIQUE

NEXT OF KIN
1414 FRANKFORD AVENUE

This easy sipper was born after a Next of Kin bar trip to New Orleans—one fueled by Sazeracs and mezcal shots at the legendary Bar Tonique. Coconut plays well with the smokiness of the mezcal, and the amaro and bitter combo rounds it all out. The team especially loves it in the summertime. A sous vide device comes in handy for the infusion but is not necessary.

GLASSWARE: Rocks glass

- Absinthe, for the wash
- 2 oz. Coconut-Infused Mezcal (see recipe)
- ¼ oz. simple syrup
- Barspoon amaro
- 3 dashes Peychaud's bitters

1. Chill a rocks glass. Coat the chilled glass with absinthe and add a big ice cube.
2. Combine the remaining ingredients in a mixing glass, add ice, and stir.
3. Strain the cocktail into the prepared glass.

Coconut-Infused Mezcal: Warm up 67.5 grams coconut oil. In a vacuum seal bag, combine the coconut oil, 1 (750 ml) bottle of mezcal, and 45 grams unsweetened coconut flakes. Seal, then place the bag in a sous vide at 144°F (62.1°C) for 3 hours. (Alternatively, combine the ingredients in an airtight container and allow to infuse for 48 hours at room temperature.) Freeze the container and its contents for 3 hours, or until the oil solidifies. Remove the container from the freezer, strain the mezcal through a coffee filter, and rebottle.

BRANDON THRASH, MIDDLE CHILD CLUBHOUSE

Brandon Thrash is the beverage director and general manager of Middle Child Clubhouse.

How did you get started in the industry? And in Philadelphia specifically?

I paid my way through college with my first job as a server and then bartender at Logan's Roadhouse in Fayetteville, Arkansas. After I graduated, I had to make a decision to either get an office job or jump headfirst into restaurants, so I picked up and drove to San Francisco with everything I owned to pursue a career. After a few years in San Francisco, I took a break to hike the Appalachian Trail, and I popped into Philadelphia on that trip. After a few days, I knew this was home, and I moved here after the trip in 2015. I've moved around a little bit since then with time in Chicago and Oregon, but Philadelphia is and will always be home.

What do you enjoy most about Middle Child?

After spending over a decade in the industry, I was tired of how slapped together and volatile it felt all the time. I wanted a place that was people first—a place that truly cared about the well-being and future of its employees and made decisions centered around that idea. I found that when I joined Middle Child Clubhouse in 2021. Every discussion was centered on how it would impact the employee, not on how it would impact the bottom line. I was sold from that moment forward.

What do you enjoy most about bartending?

I like that I get to work while also just hanging out and talking to my friends and people. Having a moment with a stranger standing across from you is so special, and you get to experience it again and again when you are a bartender.

What tips and tricks do you have for home bartenders? Is there a secret to making a great cocktail?

Don't over-dilute your cocktails. I know I'll get dragged for this in the bartending community, but technique matters more than brands—always. So ice matters. Glass temperature matters. Not over- or under-shaking or stirring your cocktails matters. I'd say that 90 percent of all cocktails at home could be made exponentially better just by freezing your glass and not using ice from your refrigerator ice machine.

What do you enjoy most about the Philadelphia cocktail community?

Philly is small enough to still feel familiar and communal, while big enough to drive innovation and creativity. There's a ton of talent here and wonderful bar teams, but none of them are so pretentious that they won't share information or their talents with other teams in the community. I love that.

SEAWATER MARGARITA

MIDDLE CHILD CLUBHOUSE
1232 NORTH FRONT STREET

Middle Child Clubhouse owner Matt Cahn and beverage director/general manager Brandon Thrash share an affinity for American highway culture, including the roadside diners and seafood shacks they remember eating at during family trips growing up in the South and mid-Atlantic. The Seawater Margarita was born out of a discussion about what a Margarita would taste like if it was made at one of those classic East Coast stops. The cocktail takes the iconic Paloma framework of grapefruit and tequila and combines it with the salinity and savory profile of kombu and celery, creating a familiar but unique twist on a favorite.

GLASSWARE: Rocks glass
GARNISH: Dehydrated grapefruit half-moon

- 2 oz. Kombu Broth (see recipe)
- 1¾ oz. Cascahuín Tequila Blanco
- ½ oz. Giffard Crème de Pamplemousse Rose
- ½ oz. Simple Syrup (see recipe on page 11)
- ½ oz. fresh lime juice
- ½ oz. grapefruit juice
- 2 dashes celery bitters

1. Combine all of the ingredients in a cocktail shaker with ice and shake.
2. Strain the cocktail over ice into a rocks glass, then garnish with a dehydrated grapefruit half-moon.

KOMBU BROTH: In a blender, combine 750 grams (750 ml) water, 250 grams celery, roughly chopped, 3 grams kombu, 2 grams salt, and 2 whole bay leaves and blend.

PILKARZ

LITTLE WALTER'S
2049 EAST HAGERT STREET

Chef and owner Michael Brenfleck names all of his cocktails after a Polish profession—and this Dirty Martini riff uses the Polish word for "footballer." In particular, this drink is inspired by a footballer's need for electrolytes. Back in 2001, Philadelphia Eagles running back Duce Staley famously drank pickle juice to avoid cramps during a 100°F game in Dallas—rushing for more than two hundred yards in the process.

GLASSWARE: Martini glass
GARNISH: Small pickle coin

- 2½ oz. Polish vodka
- ½ oz. pickle juice

1. Chill a martini glass. Pour the vodka and then the pickle juice into a cocktail shaker filled with ice.
2. Shake vigorously for about 10 seconds.
3. Strain into the chilled martini glass, and garnish with a small pickle coin.

LOLLOVE VILLAGE

CALETTA
1401 EAST SUSQUEHANNA AVENUE

This clarified rum cocktail is the work of Caletta beverage director Benjamin Kirk. It carries characteristics of two iconic drinks—the Pornstar Martini and the Piña Colada. Kirk wanted to create something that embodied his love for rum drinks. The clarified approach, while labor intensive, adds depth and texture that serves to brighten the flavors and give a smooth and elegant finish.

GLASSWARE: Highball glass
GARNISH: Grated white chocolate, slice of dehydrated passion fruit

- 1½ oz. White Chocolate Rum (see recipe)
- ½ oz. Chinola Passion Fruit Liqueur
- 1 teaspoon Giffard Vanille de Madagascar
- 1 oz. pineapple juice
- ¾ oz. fresh lime juice
- ½ oz. Passion Fruit-Coconut Syrup (see recipe)
- 17 oz. coconut milk
- Prosecco, to top

1. Combine all of the ingredients, except for the coconut milk and prosecco, in a quart-sized kitchen storage container.
2. Start the clarification process by adding 17 oz. coconut milk to the mixture and let the mixture sit for at least 30 minutes.
3. Strain first with a nut milk bag and then a coffee filter.
4. Pour the cocktail into a highball glass filled with ice. Top with prosecco.
5. Garnish with grated white chocolate and a slice of dehydrated passion fruit.

WHITE CHOCOLATE RUM: Gently melt 240 grams white chocolate, then combine it with 1 (750 ml) bottle of Planteray 3 Stars Rum in a large kitchen storage container. Freeze overnight. Fine-strain, discarding the solids.

PASSION FRUIT-COCONUT SYRUP: In a saucepan over medium-low heat, combine 1 cup sugar and 1 cup coconut milk and stir until the sugar is dissolved. Remove the mixture from heat and allow it to cool. Add 1 cup passion fruit puree and stir.

BASTIA SPRITZ

BASTIA
1401 EAST SUSQUEHANNA AVENUE

Beverage director Benjamin Kirk says that the Bastia Spritz was born from a desire to elevate the classic spritz blueprint with a little more complexity, depth, and savoriness beneath the surface. While Aperol is often the go-to for a bright, slightly bitter aperitif, Kirk swaps it out for Mazzura, which he notes offers a touch more bitterness and a richer, more robust profile while still holding onto the refreshing, citrus-forward qualities that make a spritz so invigorating. To further develop the complexity, Kirk introduces a bay leaf-infused Cocchi Americano for a subtle herbaceous note that plays off the olive brine. Black lemon bitters tie everything together, adding a unique citrus depth that enhances both the bitterness and the savory notes.

GLASSWARE: Wineglass
GARNISH: Lemon wheel, mandarin orange wheel, 2 bay leaves, 2 olives

- 1½ oz. Aperitivo Mazzura
- ½ oz. Bay Leaf–Infused Cocchi Americano (see recipe)
- 1 teaspoon olive brine
- Dash black lemon bitters
- 1 oz. Perrier Sparkling Natural Mineral Water
- 3 oz. prosecco

1. Build all of the ingredients directly into a wineglass filled with ice. Give it a quick swizzle or stir.

2. Garnish with a lemon wheel and mandarin orange wheel, 2 bay leaves, and 2 olives.

BAY LEAF–INFUSED COCCHI AMERICANO: Combine 6 bay leaves and 350 ml Cocchi Americano in a Cryovac bag and sous vide for 2 hours at 140°F (60°C). (Alternatively, let the infusion sit in the refrigerator for 1 week, shaking a couple times a day.) Strain.

GREEN LIGHT

ST. ONER'S
2218 FRANKFORD AVENUE

This refreshing and easy-to-build Highball is a hybrid of a Mojito and a Margarita. Mint and cucumber bring a green freshness, and the tequila base gives a sweet and citrusy brightness.

GLASSWARE: Highball or stemless wineglass
GARNISH: Mint leaves

- Bunch mint leaves
- 1½ oz. tequila
- ½ oz. Simple Syrup (see recipe on page 11)
- ½ oz. triple sec
- 1 oz. cucumber juice
- ¾ oz. fresh lime juice
- Soda water, to top

1. Muddle the mint in a cocktail shaker.
2. Fill the shaker with ice and add the remaining ingredients, except for the soda water.
3. Shake well, about 10 seconds.
4. Strain the cocktail into a glass filled with fresh ice, and top with soda water.
5. Garnish with mint leaves.

SOULMONGER

ST. ONER'S
2218 FRANKFORD AVENUE

Whiskey brings the strength, apple cider's acidity is tempered by reducing the cider into a rich syrup, and an array of citrus and herbal flavors create interest in this Old Fashioned-like concoction.

GLASSWARE: Rocks glass
GARNISH: Lemon peel, expressed

- 2 oz. rye whiskey
- 2 dashes absinthe
- ¾ oz. Apple Cider Syrup (see recipe)
- 1 oz. fresh lemon juice
- 3 dashes Peychaud's bitters
- 2 dashes Angostura bitters

1. Combine all of the ingredients, except for the Angostura bitters, in a cocktail shaker with ice and shake well, about 10 seconds.
2. Add 1 large ice cube to a rocks glass.
3. Double-strain the cocktail into the glass.
4. Add 2 dashes of Angostura bitters.
5. Express a lemon peel over the rim and place it on top of the ice cube.

APPLE CIDER SYRUP: In a pot over medium-low heat, combine 1 cup apple cider and 1 cup white sugar. Heat gradually and stir until the sugar is dissolved. Allow the mixture to cool before use.

THE PLEASURE CLUB OF FIUMEDINISI

CICALA
699 NORTH BROAD STREET

This play on a Clover Club, historically a Philadelphia cocktail, is a nod to chef Joe Cicala's Washingtonion and Sicilian roots. The drink's namesake was a lodge and social club in the Maryland suburbs of DC, formed by Sicilian immigrants in 1923 and named after the Cicala family village of Fiumedinisi. The lodge held dances and meetings, had a social area for card games, homemade wine and beer, courts for bocce, as well as a greased pole to challenge the climbing abilities of young men during weekend parties.

GLASSWARE: Coupe glass
GARNISH: 5 drops Peychaud's bitters

- 1 oz. egg white
- ½ oz. clementine juice
- ¼ oz. blood orange juice
- ¼ oz. dry vermouth
- 1½ oz. barrel-aged gin

1. Chill a coupe glass. Combine all of the ingredients, except for the gin, in a cocktail shaker without ice and dry-shake.
2. Add the gin and ice and shake again, for about 10 seconds.
3. Double-strain the cocktail into the chilled coupe, then garnish with 5 drops of Peychaud's bitters, dragging a toothpick across the tops to make hearts.

JOSETTE BONAFINO AND IAN CROSS, THE TRESTLE INN

Trestle Inn co-owners Josette Bonafino and Ian Cross met in 1991 when Josette was editor of *The Intercollegiate*, a monthly arts-and-entertainment tabloid for Philadelphia-area college students, and Ian was a staff music writer.

Now married, the couple and self-described "nightlifers" own and operate the iconic bar and entertainment venue once the notorious corner strip club known as the J & J Trestle Inn. It's their first foray into bar ownership.

The couple bought the dilapidated building nestled under the now-defunct Reading Railroad in 2003 and lovingly restored it, paying homage to the old strip club and the "sound of Philadelphia," the internationally known soul music that emerged from Philadelphia's inner city in the 1960s and 1970s. It was music they both loved as kids. The reimagined Trestle Inn opened in 2011 with the tagline "Whiskey and Go Go," a reference to their era of inspiration. To this day, guests are still coming to the bar to realize that "Go Go" doesn't mean "strip" but rather dancers in fringe costumes shimmying to soul, funk, and disco on illuminated boxes.

For the spirits and cocktails, Bonafino and Cross focused on developing an extensive menu of affordable bourbons, ryes, and international whiskeys. They also decided to bring back the Whiskey Sour, a drink popular in the 1960s. They elevated the classic cocktail back to its original late nineteenth-century recipe using fresh lemon juice (rather than a sour mix) and egg white foam. The Whiskey Sour remains the signature cocktail of The Trestle Inn.

Other house-designed Whiskey Sour riffs on 1960s and 1970s culture include the Pink Panther Sour, made with 100-proof bourbon, raspberry puree, pink peppercorn mint syrup, fresh lemon juice, a dash of Galliano, and garnished with mint leaves.

The Trestle Inn is open Thursday to Saturday, featuring all-vinyl DJs and Go Go dancers nightly.

CLASSIC WHISKEY SOUR

THE TRESTLE INN
339 NORTH 11TH STREET

The Trestle Inn is known around Philadelphia for its signature Whiskey Sour. Owners Josette Bonafino and Ian Cross have a great respect for the 1960s-era classic. In addition to cocktails, the Trestle Inn bar is stocked with an extensive menu of affordable bourbons, ryes, and international whiskeys.

GLASSWARE: Rocks glass
GARNISH: Lemon peel

- 1½ oz. Four Roses Bourbon
- 1 oz. Simple Syrup (see recipe on page 11)
- 1 oz. fresh lemon juice
- 1 egg white

1. Add the bourbon, simple syrup, and lemon juice to the small side of a cocktail tin.
2. Add the egg white to the large side of the cocktail tin.
3. Dry-shake (without ice) vigorously.
4. Open the tins, add ice, and wet-shake until chilled.
5. Strain the cocktail into a large rocks glass. Add ice and garnish with a lemon peel.

SOUL FASHIONED

THE TRESTLE INN
339 NORTH 11TH STREET

The Trestle Inn developed this specialty cocktail specifically for Uncle Nearest, a black female–owned distillery. Sales of this cocktail were used to raise money for Historically Black Colleges and Universities (HBCUs). Here, the blueprint for the standard whiskey Old Fashioned gets amplified by a sweet and earthy golden beet syrup as well as a touch of smoke aroma from a mezcal rinse.

GLASSWARE: Rocks glass
GARNISH: Orange coin

- Ilegal Mezcal Joven, for the rinse
- 2 oz. Uncle Nearest 1884 Small Batch Whiskey
- Barspoon Golden Beet Syrup (see recipe)
- Dash Tasmania Bitters Mountain Pepperberry

1. Rinse a rocks glass with the mezcal. Combine the remaining ingredients in a mixing glass with ice.
2. Stir until well chilled.
3. Strain the cocktail into the rocks glass, filled with a couple of big ice cubes.
4. Use a candle or match to light a bamboo skewer, then use the lit skewer to express an orange coin over the drink. Then add the orange coin as a garnish.

GOLDEN BEET SYRUP: Clean 5 to 6 golden beets and pat them dry. Toss the beets in a bowl with olive oil, as needed, a few dashes kosher salt, and few dashes white pepper. Wrap each seasoned beet separately and tightly in a tin foil packet and place on a tray in an oven preheated to 400°F. Roast for 45 to 90 minutes, checking every 20 minutes; the beets are done when a fork or skewer slides easily to the center of the beet. Allow the beets to cool at room temperature in tin foil overnight. Unwrap and peel the beets. Weigh the beets then add them to a blender. Add an equal weight of turbinado sugar and blend until smooth. Add 2 oz. maple syrup and blend again.

RIDIN' DIRTY

LA CHINESCA
1036 SPRING GARDEN STREET

The Dirty Martini gets some Chinese flair with the Ridin' Dirty. Created by Derek Gregory's director of operations for the 13th Street Kitchens hospitality group, the cocktail gets savory notes from a shaoxing wine-olive brine mix and an MSG solution that compliments La Chinesca's Mexicali cooking.

GLASSWARE: Coupe
GARNISH: Olives on a skewer

- 2½ oz. Tito's Handmade Vodka
- ½ oz. olive brine
- ¼ oz. shaoxing wine
- 4 drops MSG Solution (see recipe)

1. Combine all of the ingredients in a cocktail shaker with ice.
2. Shake until well chilled and combined, about 10 seconds.
3. Strain the cocktail into a coupe and garnish with olives on a skewer.

MSG SOLUTION: In a jar, combine 90 grams water and 10 grams MSG powder and stir until the powder is dissolved. Use with a dropper bottle.

CELEBRITY SKIN

POISON HEART
931 SPRING GARDEN STREET

"Celebrity Skin" is the title track of a record by the 1990s band Hole that is a favorite of the staff at Poison Heart. "We wanted to do a Naked and Famous riff that was served on the rocks," says Amanda Moore, a close friend of the Poison Heart team who helped create the original Poison Heart cocktail program. Centerbe is "a little less viscous than Chartreuse," she says but still adds the green color.

GLASSWARE: Rocks glass
GARNISH: Mint bouquet

- 1¼ oz. espadín mezcal
- 1 oz. pineapple juice
- ¾ oz. John D. Taylor's Velvet Falernum
- ½ oz. Dolin Génépy le Chamois Liqueur
- ½ oz. fresh lime juice
- ¼ oz. Centerbe Faccia Brutto
- 2 dashes Bittermens Hellfire Habanero Shrub Bitters
- Pinch sea salt

1. Combine all of the ingredients in a cocktail shaker with both large and crushed ice cubes.
2. Shake with until chilled.
3. Strain the cocktail over fresh ice into a large rocks glass and garnish with a mint bouquet.

BITCHIN' CAMARO

POISON HEART
931 SPRING GARDEN STREET

During her time at Poison Heart, bartender (and still close friend of the team) Liv Arterbridge went through several iterations before landing on the recipe for the Bitchin' Camaro, including a "too funky" version with overproof rhum agricole. Owner and manager Andrea Ulsh calls it one of those drinks that's "a little weird." The spirit-forward tiki cocktail takes its name from a song by The Dead Milkmen—and it's also an excuse for the bar to use its pebble ice machine.

GLASSWARE: Collins glass
GARNISH: Lime wheel, Luxardo cherry, umbrella

- 1 oz. El Dorado 5 Year Old Rum
- ½ oz. Giffard Banane du Brésil
- ½ oz. Cappelletti
- ½ oz. Coco López Cream of Coconut
- ½ oz. fresh lime juice
- ½ oz. pineapple juice
- ¼ oz. Smith & Cross Jamaica Rum
- 2 dashes Angostura bitters

1. Combine all of the ingredients in a cocktail shaker with large ice cubes.
2. Shake until chilled.
3. Strain the cocktail over pebble ice into a collins glass.
4. Garnish with a lime wheel, Luxardo cherry, and umbrella.

IT'S ALL GUAVA, BABY

LMNO
1739-1749 NORTH FRONT STREET

Take a page from LMNO's agave-heavy cocktail list with this rose-colored highball of tequila, guava, and strawberry. It's fruity, citrusy, with a touch of bitterness coming from the Aperol. The extra effort of crafting a strawberry salt rim adds a finishing sweet and savory note.

GLASSWARE: Collins glass
GARNISH: Lime wedge

- Strawberry Salt (see recipe), for the rim
- 1½ oz. Corazón Blanco Tequila
- 1 oz. Aperol
- 1 oz. fresh lime juice
- ½ oz. Guava Paste Syrup (see recipe)
- ½ oz. strawberry puree

1. Wet the rim of a collins glass with a lime wedge and then dip the glass in the Strawberry Salt to give it a rim.
2. Combine the remaining ingredients in a cocktail shaker with ice and shake well, until combined and chilled.
3. Strain the cocktail into the rimmed glass filled with fresh ice. Garnish with a lime wedge.

STRAWBERRY SALT: Muddle 60 grams Maldon Sea Salt Flakes and 2 grams freeze-dried strawberries together until the larger flakes are broken down.

GUAVA PASTE SYRUP: In a glass container, combine 1 cup guava paste and 1 cup hot water and blend with an immersion blender until smooth. Alternatively, combine the ingredients in a saucepan over low heat and stir.

OUR DAILY VEDGE

LMNO
1739-1749 NORTH FRONT STREET

Fishtown's LMNO combines Mexican restaurant with 1970s-style cocktail lounge and art space. Our Daily Vedge is here to be a cocktail with a little less guilt attached to it, and a lot of flavor. Earthy notes from mezcal provide the punch to house-made green juice.

GLASSWARE: Rocks glass
GARNISH: Celery, onion, and tomato on a skewer

- 1½ oz. Green Juice (see recipe)
- 1½ oz. Mezcal Apaluz Joven
- ¾ oz. fresh lemon juice
- ½ oz. Ancho Reyes Verde Chile Poblano Liqueur
- ½ oz. Corn Husk Syrup (see recipe)

1. Combine all ingredients together in a mixing glass filled with ice and stir until well chilled.
2. Strain the cocktail into a rocks glass over ice.
3. Garnish with celery, onion, and a tomato on a skewer.

GREEN JUICE: In a blender, combine 2½ green bell peppers, stems and seeds removed; 2½ tomatillos, wrappings removed and rinsed; 1½ nopales paddles; 1 poblano pepper, and 1 English cucumber and blend. Fine-strain.

CORN HUSK SYRUP: In a container, combine 5 oz. warm corn husk broth (left over from boiling corn) and 5 oz. sugar and stir until dissolved.

BLOOD, SWEAT, AND CHEERS

STATESIDE VODKA DISTILLERY
1700 NORTH HANCOCK STREET

Don't call it a Margarita, but this shaken vodka drink has similar traits. A blood orange–infused vodka mixes with orange liqueur, lime, agave, and a splash of pomegranate juice for a citrusy, colorful cocktail that's simple to whip up and even easier to enjoy.

GLASSWARE: Rocks glass
GARNISH: Lime wheel

- 1½ oz. Blood Orange–Infused Vodka (see recipe)
- ½ oz. orange liqueur
- 1 oz. pomegranate juice
- ¼ oz. fresh lime juice
- ¼ oz. agave nectar
- Salt, for the rim

1. Combine all of the ingredients, except for the salt, in a cocktail shaker filled with ice and shake well, about 10 seconds.
2. Rim a rocks glass with salt, using a lime wedge to help the salt stick.
3. Strain the cocktail into the rimmed rocks glass over fresh ice.
4. Garnish with a lime wheel.

BLOOD ORANGE–INFUSED VODKA: In a large jar or kitchen storage container, combine 1 (750 ml) bottle of Stateside Urbancraft Vodka and 1 blood orange, sliced. Let the mixture infuse for 3 to 5 days. Strain and rebottle.

GETTIN' CHILI OUT

**STATESIDE VODKA DISTILLERY
1700 NORTH HANCOCK STREET**

This frothy sipper brings a little sweetness and a little spice, along with a bright and fruity backbone from lime and pineapple juice. A vanilla-infused vodka does much of the lifting. It's a straightforward recipe, but does take some planning ahead, as the infusion requires several days to steep. The spice level in the chile simple syrup can be dialed in based on personal preference. A little goes a long way.

GLASSWARE: Coupe glass
GARNISH: Dried chile pepper

- 1 egg white
- 1½ oz. Vanilla-Infused Vodka (see recipe)
- ½ oz. pineapple juice
- ¼ oz. fresh lime juice
- ¼ oz. Calabrian Chile Simple Syrup (see recipe)

1. Dry-shake (no ice) the egg white in a cocktail tin.
2. Add the remaining ingredients, along with ice, and shake well until chilled and combined.
3. Strain the cocktail into a coupe and serve with a dried chile pepper.

VANILLA-INFUSED VODKA: Combine 1 (750 ml) bottle of Stateside Urbancraft Vodka and 2 vanilla beans, sliced, in a large jar or kitchen storage container. Let the mixture infuse for 3 to 5 days. Strain and rebottle.

CALABRIAN CHILE SIMPLE SYRUP: In a small saucepan over medium-low heat, combine ½ cup water, ½ cup white sugar, and ¼ teaspoon pureed Calabrian chile pepper and simmer, stirring until the sugar is dissolved. Strain and allow the syrup to cool.

FRED BEEBE, POST HASTE

Post Haste opened in East Kensington in 2023 with a farm-to-glass beverage philosophy. The entire bar, from spirits and wines to citrus and herbs, is sourced exclusively from east of the Mississippi.

"The idea is to not beat people over the head with our ethics, because if sustainable, locally focused practices are going to become the norm they can't just be a trendy selling point," says partner and beverage director Fred Beebe, who owns the bar with longtime friend Gabriel Guerrero.

Beebe and Guerrero co-founded a 100% local, 90% organic cafe during their college years. That venture was the starting point for Post Haste's ethos of sustainability and local sourcing across beverage and culinary programs. Those ideals mean the team has to work with the growing seasons and harvest times for fresh ingredients. To accomplish this, the bar orders in bulk during the height of the season and then preserves ingredients by freezing and infusing, and by creating rich syrups.

The Post Haste drink menu is sorted into categories based around different types of songs. It begins with "Covers"—drinks inspired by classic cocktails. That's Fashion, Baby! is a spirit-forward sip of rye whiskey and Laird's Straight Apple Brandy Bottled in Bond, a Philadelphia favorite. "Remixes" are reimaginings or abstract renditions of familiar cocktails. Cocktails listed under "Experimental Pop" are more adventurous and limited offerings, with rare ingredients like foraged cardoon thistle.

Although the phrase, "post-haste," signals a sense of urgency, Bebee says he wants the bar to be the place to unwind after a busy day. "The most important experience is having a great night away from your troubles and worries," he says.

BAY SIDE SNAP

POST HASTE
2519 FRANKFORD AVENUE

While Bay Side Snap seems like a variation of the New York Sour, Post Haste co-owner and bartender Fred Beebe says it's actually an updated version of the Claret Snap, which was invented in Chicago in the late 1800s. Claret (a British term for wines from Bordeaux) was a popular style of red wine at the time and was added as a red wine float on Whiskey Sours. Fitting with the bar's focus on sustainability, this recipe takes advantage of the fact that kumquats are wholly edible with no pith.

GLASSWARE: Rocks glass
GARNISH: Red Wine Foam (see recipe)

- 1½ oz. bottled-in-bond bourbon
- ½ oz. rye whiskey
- 1 oz. Bay Leaf Syrup (see recipe)
- ¾ oz. Kumquat Superjuice (see recipe)

1. Combine all of the ingredients in a cocktail shaking tin with one large ice cube and 2 to 3 small cubes and shake for 10 to 12 seconds.
2. Strain the cocktail into chilled double rocks glass with no ice (serve up).
3. Garnish with a flow of Red Wine Foam.

BAY LEAF SYRUP: Combine 250 grams boiling water, 250 grams sugar, and 5 grams fresh bay leaves and let the mixture steep for 1 hour before straining and storing in the refrigerator.

Kumquat Superjuice: Juice 1 pound kumquats, reserving both the pulp and the juice. A macerating juicer is great for this, but any juicer will work. Cover the pulp with 45 grams of citric acid in a coverable container. Shake to evenly distribute the acid, and then let sit for 1 hour. Add the citric acid/pulp mixture, the kumquat juice, and 26 oz. water to a blender. Blend on high for 1 minute, and then strain through a fine-mesh strainer.

Red Wine Foam: In an iSi canister, combine 1 (750 ml) bottle of local, light-bodied, and fruit-forward red wine with 7.5 grams Modernist Pantry Foam Magic. Charge twice with N_2O canisters, shaking for 20 seconds between charges.

THAT'S FASHION BABY!

POST HASTE
2519 FRANKFORD AVENUE

The flavors of this cocktail come in part from burnt sugar cake, a recipe that dates back to the Great Depression, if not before. As Post Haste co-owner and bartender Fred Beebe explains it, toasting and burning the sugar for additional flavor was a great trick for those who didn't have a lot of money or ingredients but had the most important thing for this recipe: time. It's a slow process of constantly stirring the sugar while it browns, resulting in a rich, dark syrup with nutty, smoky notes. The syrup, combined with red wine vinegar, becomes agrodolce, a savory, rich, and tangy sweetener.

GLASSWARE: Double rocks glass

- ¼ oz. Red Wine & Burnt Sugar Agrodolce (see recipe)
- 1 oz. Laird's Straight Apple Brandy Bottled in Bond
- 1 oz. Rittenhouse Straight Rye Whisky
- 2 dashes Fee Brothers Black Walnut Bitters

1. Combine all of the ingredients, in the order listed, in a mixing glass.
2. Add ice and stir until properly diluted and chilled, usually around 30 to 45 seconds.
3. Strain the cocktail into a double rocks glass over a large cube.

RED WINE & BURNT SUGAR AGRODOLCE: In a pot over medium-low heat, combine 450 grams white sugar, 1 cup water, ⅓ cup red wine vinegar, ⅓ cup sweet vermouth, ⅓ cup maple syrup, and ⅛ teaspoon salt. Bring to a low simmer for 20 minutes. Pour the mixture into a separate container and set aside. Bring 2 cups water to a boil in an electric kettle and set aside. In a clean pot over medium heat, add 450 grams white sugar and cook until the sugar begins to melt. Stir the sugar constantly to prevent burning, and to integrate the melted sugar. Once the sugar is golden brown in color, bring your water to a boil again, and then slowly pour 1 cup water over the golden sugar, stirring to integrate. Bring the sugar and water to a simmer for 20 minutes, stirring occasionally to break down the sugar solids. Add the red wine-and-vermouth mixture back into the burnt sugar syrup and stir to integrate. Simmer this mixture for an additional 30 minutes, making sure it doesn't boil , then allow it to cool.

KASUGAI SOUR

ALMANAC
310 MARKET STREET

This drink takes its name from Kasugai Confectionery, a large candy producer in Japan. Almanac head bartender Rob Scott remembers family trips to the local sushi joint, where he'd grab a melon flavored candy Kasugai on the way out. Those childhood memories are recreated here in an easy-to-execute recipe that builds on a base of Japanese shochu.

GLASSWARE: Coupe glass
GARNISH: Dehydrated lime wheel

- 1½ oz. Yanagita Aokage 41 Shochu
- ¾ oz. Midori
- ½ oz. yuzu juice
- ½ oz. fresh lime juice
- ¾ oz. CALPICO Concentrate

1. Combine all of the ingredients in a cocktail shaker with ice and shake hard for 8 to 10 seconds.
2. Double-strain the cocktail into a coupe and garnish with a dehydrated lime wheel.

SADŌTINI

ALMANAC
310 MARKET STREET

Almanac's cocktails were developed by James Beard Award–winning author Danny Childs. His book, *Slow Drinks*, explores the practice of foraging and transforming seasonal botanicals and ingredients into beverages through natural techniques like fermentation. Here, Sadōtini refers to the "Way of the Tea," or the Japanese tea ceremony. Head bartender Rob Scott and the Almanac team make matcha a la minute with a *chasen* (tea whisk) and a *chawan* (tea bowl) for the freshest possible result. The star ingredient is amazake, a traditional Japanese fermented rice drink. A bit of patience is required, but the final product makes for an excellent warm and hearty sip in the cold months or, served chilled, a refreshing one in the summertime.

GLASSWARE: Coupe glass
GARNISH: Sifted matcha powder

- 1½ oz. Amazake (see recipe)
- 1 oz. freshly brewed matcha
- ¾ oz. Natsu No Mannen Imo Shōchū
- ¾ oz. Roku Gin
- ½ oz. Haku Vodka
- ¼ oz. Rich Simple Syrup (see recipe on page 11)
- 1 egg white

1. Combine all of the ingredients in a cocktail shaker and dry-shake (no ice) until the egg white is emulsified.
2. Add ice and shake hard for 8 to 10 seconds.
3. Double-strain the cocktail into a large coupe and garnish with sifted matcha powder.

AMAZAKE: Make 1 cup short-grain rice with 3 cups water according to the porridge settings on a rice cooker. (Alternatively, cook 1 cup white rice and 3 cups water in a pot on the stove.) This will create a loose rice porridge. Remove from heat, add 1 cup water, and let the mixture sit until it has cooled to around 130°F (koji cannot survive above 140°F.) Add 1 cup dried koji (komekoji) and mix thoroughly. Keep the mixture between 130°F and 140°F for 8 hours with a sous vide held precisely to 135°F, placing the amazake mixture in a mason jar loosely covered. If you do not have a sous vide, you can use the "keep warm" function on a rice cooker, or use a pot on the stove at a low simmer. The rice porridge mixture will have a sweet and slightly tangy smell from the fermentation from the koji. Blend and store in the refrigerator for up to a month.

PAUL MACDONALD, FRIDAY SATURDAY SUNDAY

Head bartender at Friday Saturday Sunday Paul MacDonald crafts drinks using a standard recipe ratio based on the Fibonnaci sequence. The idea, at first, was to build a cocktail from five contrasting fortified wines, with their flavors arranged in such a way that they would present successively across the palate to create a long, meandering flavor profile. That original drink consisted of Sercial Madeira, Quinquina, Punt e Mes, Cardamaro, and Torino Vermouth in ratios that modeled the Fibonacci sequence—¼ oz., ¼ oz., ½ oz., ¾ oz., and 1¼ oz.

"It led me to experiment extensively with different combinations that could fit into the same mold," MacDonald said.

This reverse-engineered approach to cocktail construction, going ratio first rather than ingredient first, has turned MacDonald on to a few surprising flavor combinations that he says he might otherwise never have explored. "It has pushed me over the years to fundamentally rethink my approach to cocktail flavor constructions. Probably the two most enduringly popular Fibonacci Cocktails have been The War on Christmas and Being Frank," he says.

THE WAR ON CHRISTMAS

FRIDAY SATURDAY SUNDAY
261 SOUTH 21ST STREET

This stirred cocktail follows bartender Paul MacDonald's ratio for building drinks. Aquavit's notes of rye spice, citrus, and anise uplift this balanced sipper. It falls together with Cardamaro, dry madeira, and bittersweet citrus coming from orange liqueur and the specific amaro.

GLASSWARE: Rocks glass
GARNISH: Orange peel, sage leaf

- 1¼ oz. Brennivín Aquavit
- ¾ oz. Cardamaro
- ½ oz. Henriques & Henriques 5-Year Special Dry Madeira
- ¼ oz. Rhum J.M Shrubb Liqueur d'Orange
- ¼ oz. Amaro Ramazzotti

1. Combine all of the ingredients in a mixing glass with ice.
2. Stir well until combined, chilled, and diluted, about 10 to 15 seconds.
3. Strain the cocktail into a rocks glass over one large ice cube. Garnish with an orange peel and a sage leaf.

HIGHWAY ROBBERY

IZZY'S COCKTAIL BAR
35 EAST LANCASTER AVENUE, ARDMORE

General manager and bartender Michael Haggerty calls the Highway Robbery a play on the "Si-Güey" by legendary bartender Sasha Petraske. This one gets some Japanese flair with its base of Japanese whisky and yuzu curaçao.

GLASSWARE: Nick & Nora glass
GARNISH: Smith & Cross Jamaica Rum spritz

- 2 oz. Mars Iwai 45 Whisky
- ½ oz. Pierre Ferrand Late Harvest Dry Curaçao Yuzu
- ¼ oz. Sandeman Rainwater Madeira
- Dash lavender bitters

1. Combine all of the ingredients in a cocktail mixing tin filled with ice and stir until well chilled and combined, about 10 seconds.
2. Strain the cocktail into a Nick & Nora, then garnish with a spritz of Jamaican rum.

UNTITLED

FELL TO EARTH VERMOUTH

Tim Kweeder and business partner Zach Morris started making vermouth together while working at Bloomsday Cafe. During the pandemic, the Dumpster Juice label grew into what is now Fell to Earth, a South Philadelphia distillery and winery. Kweeder crafts his vermouths from local botanicals, and Fell to Earth's products are used in cocktails at bars across Philadelphia. The team's future plans include opening a public tasting room and bar. This cocktail makes use of Pennsylvania spirits and ingredients, including a garnish of local, cold-hardy trifoliate orange and green coriander from a small farm in Lancaster. It is a savory, low-ABV stirred drink that's been featured at events and collaborative bar pop-ups around town.

GLASSWARE: Coupe glass
GARNISH: Pickled green coriander seeds

- 2½ oz. Fell to Earth Dry Vermouth
- ¼ oz. Boardroom Spirits B: Beet Eau de Vie
- ¼ oz. Revivalist Dragon Dance Jalapeño Gin
- Orange zest, to express

1. Combine all of the ingredients, except for the orange zest, in a rocks glass with 1 large ice cube.
2. Stir until combined and chilled, about 10 seconds.
3. Express the orange zest around the rim and discard the zest. Garnish with pickled green coriander seeds.

MEASUREMENT CONVERSIONS

	1 dash		0.625 ml
	4 dashes		2.5 ml
	1 teaspoon		5 ml
¼ oz.			7.5 ml
⅓ oz.	2 teaspoons		10 ml
½ oz.	3 teaspoons	1 tablespoon	15 ml
⅔ oz.	4 teaspoons		20 ml
¾ oz.			22.5 ml
17/20 oz.			25 ml
1 oz.		2 tablespoons	30 ml
1½ oz.		3 tablespoons	45 ml
1¾ oz.			52.5 ml
2 oz.	4 tablespoons	¼ cup	60 ml
8 oz.		1 cup	250 ml
16 oz.	1 pint	2 cups	500 ml
24 oz.		3 cups	750 ml
32 oz.	1 quart	4 cups	1 liter (1,000 ml)

ACKNOWLEDGMENTS

This project is a reflection of the talent and ambition of the city of Philadelphia. I would like to thank the team at HarperCollins and Cider Mill Press for entrusting me with this project and allowing me to tell these stories. There are so many people who made this project a success.

I owe much gratitude to Nico Diaz for his guidance throughout this process. Thank you for being a sounding board and for sharing your deep knowledge of and pride in the Philadelphia cocktail community. I would also like to recognize Michael McCaulley for his enthusiasm and contributions that helped this book take shape. For the second time, I am lucky to have Jeremy Hauck as my steady editor and to keep everything (especially me) on track. And thank you, as always, to my wife, Jamie Mackey, for her tireless encouragement and for being the best plus one around.

Finally, know that this book would not have been possible without the superb talent and dedication of the Philadelphia bartending family. There are simply too many worthy names to mention. I raise a glass to you all. Cheers!

ABOUT THE AUTHOR

Travis Mitchell is a D.C.-based journalist who has spent more than a decade writing about food and spirits. He is also the author of *DC Cocktails* (Cider Mill Press 2024).

PHOTO CREDITS

Page 23 Charlotte Nagey; pages 33, 37, 219, 220 Ed Newton; page 38 Adrian Garcia; page 47 Luke Kingsley; page 53 Mike Prince; page 57 Jason Varney; page 61 Jordan Harris; page 67 Julia Soniat; page 68 Michael McCaulley; page 74 Nicole Guglielmo; page 81 Chris Zingler; pages 82, 85, 153, 154, 159, 162, 165, 187, 189 Travis Mitchell; pages 86, 93, 98, 102, 131, 137, 200 Gab Bonghi; page 90 Neil Santos; page 94 Kelly McMonagle; page 101 Max Mester; page 109 Chris Harrop; pages 117, 118–119 Christopher Devern; page 121 Patrick Banko; pages 126, 129 Shawn Miller; page 138 Shelby Ricci for Reel Media Agency; page 143 Liz Wissmann; page 145 Media Kriste Jorgensen; page 150 Lexie Fleege; page 157 Kerry McKenzie; page 175 Steve Legato; pages 192, 195, 231, 233, 235 KC Tinari Photography; page 199 Michael Persico; pages 203, 205 Oliviea Kallenberger for Oakbranch Photography; pages 207, 209 Sean Arthurs; page 215 Ian Cross; pages 216–217 Deanna Leone; page 223 Alex Cahanap; pages 227, 229 Dan Heinkel; pages 236, 239 Stephen Recchia; page 243 Michael Haggerty; page 245 Tim Kweeder.

Pages 1, 3, 4–5, 6, 8, 13, 16, 18–19, 59, 104–105, 146–147, 176–177 used under official license from Shutterstock.com.

Pages 7, 12, 14, 15 courtesy of the Library of Congress.

All other images courtesy of the respective bars, restaurants, and interviewees.

INDEX

A.Bar, 76–77, 79
absinthe
  for home bar, 9
  Mutter's Charm, 184
  Soulmonger, 208
  Tonique, 194–195
agave nectar
  Agave Simple Syrup, 61
  Basil Agave Syrup, 118
  Blood, Sweat, and Cheers, 226
  Garden Smash, 118
  Margarita Vert, 60–61
  Mezcal Margarita, 40
  Paloma, 43
Agave Simple Syrup
  Margarita Vert, 60–61
  recipe, 61
Agave Vesper, 75
Almanac, 237, 238–239
almonds
  Fiori di Sicilia, 160
  Toasted Almond-Infused Bianco Vermouth, 160
amaretto
  The Butcher, 72
amaro
  Smoke & Barrels, 193
  Tonique, 194–195
Amaro Averna
  In the Body of Swan, 151
  Golden Revolver, 163
  Sacrifice to the Gods, 76–77
Amaro Meletti
  No Call, No Show, 185
Amaro Montenegro
  Charmed, I'm Sure, 29
Amaro Nardini
  BP Manhattan, 92
Amaro Nonino Quintessentia
  Scorched Atlas, 141
Amaro Ramazzotti
  The War on Christmas, 241
Amaro Sfumato Rabarbaro
  Lawless Doings, 26–27
Amazake
  recipe, 239
  Sadōtini, 238–239
American Sardine Bar, 168, 169
Ancho Reyes Verde Chile Poblano Liqueur
  Felipe Collins, 91
  Our Daily Vedge, 225

Angostura bitters
  APP Bitters, 29
  Bitchin' Camaro, 221
  Bombay Moon, 80–81
  Charmed, I'm Sure, 29
  Deranged Lumberjack Old Fashioned, 52
  Fall Seasonal Old Fashioned, 161
  Investment Manhattan, 99
  Neck Brace, 79
  Old Fashioned, 96
  Paradise Rum Punch, 114
  Sip Your Sins, 66
  Soulmonger, 208
Aperitivo Mazzura
  Bastia Spritz, 204–205
Aperol
  Garden Smash, 118
  It's All Guava, Baby, 222–223
  Mutter's Charm, 184
  Pensylvania Punch, 182
  Spritz Royale, 95
APP Bitters
  Charmed, I'm Sure, 29
  recipe, 29
apple brandy
  Apple Brandy Sidecar, 171
  In the Body of Swan, 151
  That's Fashion Baby! 234–235
Apple Cider Syrup
  recipe, 208
  Soulmonger, 208
Apple Cordial
  Pear of Apples, 110–111
apples
  Apple Cordial, 110
  Granny Smith Apple Cordial, 33
  Pear of Apples, 110–111
  Waiting for the Moon to Rise, 32–33
aquavit
  The War on Christmas, 241
Armagnac
  The Butcher, 72
Arterbrider, Liv, 221
Astronaut, 87
Awaji-Musubi, 69
Balsamic Syrup
  Kimono Racer, 73
  recipe, 73
Bamonte, Jon, 39
Banhez Ensamble
  Mezcal Margarita, 40

Bar Lesieur, 58–59, 60–61
Barclay Prime, 92
Bartender for Hire, 116–117
basil
  Basil Agave Syrup, 118
  Garden Smash, 118
  Strawberry Street, 136–137
Bastia, 204–205
Bastia Spritz, 204–205
Bay Leaf Syrup
  Bay Side Snap, 232–233
  recipe, 232
Bay Leaf–Infused Cocchi Americano
  Bastia Spritz, 204–205
  recipe, 205
Bay Side Snap, 232–233
Beebe, Fred, 230, 232–233, 234–235
beer
  The Special, 155
beets
  Beet It, 108–109
  Beet-and-Carrot Gin Infusion, 109
  Golden Beet Syrup, 215
  Soul Fashioned, 214–215
Best Served Cold 2.0, 36–37
Bitchin' Camaro, 221
black walnut bitters
  That's Fashion Baby! 234–235
Blood, Sweat, and Cheers, 226
blood oranges/blood orange juice
  Blood, Sweat, and Cheers, 226
  Blood Orange–Infused Vodka, 226
  Frozen Blood Orange Margarita, 88
  The Pleasure Club of Fiumedinisi, 210
blueberries
  The Boog, 139
Bob & Barbara's Lounge, 152–153, 155
Bolo, 103
Bolo's Coconut Cream
  Piña Colada, 103
  recipe, 103
Bombay Moon, 80–81
Bonafino, Josette, 212, 213
Bonal Gentiane-Quina
  In the Body of Swan, 151
  Scorched Atlas, 141
Boog, The, 139
BOTLD Midtown, 52
bourbon
  Bartender for Hire, 116–117

PHILADELPHIA COCKTAILS — 249

Bay Side Snap, 232–233
Bombay Moon, 80–81
The Boog, 139
Carrot Me Home, 124–125
Chai Tea–Infused Bourbon, 161
Classic Whiskey Sour, 213
Deranged Lumberjack Old Fashioned, 52
Fall Seasonal Old Fashioned, 161
Golden Revolver, 163
Lemonana, 142
Sip Your Sins, 66
The Special, 155
Strawberry Street, 136–137
BP Manhattan, 92
Brander, Tom, 70–71, 72
brandy
  Fish House Punch, 39
  Peach Brandy, 39
brandy, apple
  Apple Brandy Sidecar, 171
  In the Body of Swan, 151
  That's Fashion Baby! 234–235
Braulio Amaro
  Rocket Fuel, 140
Brenfleck, Michael, 201
Brennivin
  Best Served Cold 2.0, 36–37
Butcher, The, 72
Butcher and Singer, 96, 99
Byrne, Sean, 185
Byrrh Grand Quinquina aperitif
  Awaji-Musubi, 69
Cacao Nibs–Infused Rum
  recipe, 35
  The Sacred Cow, 34–35
cactus pear puree
  Prickly Pear Wasabi Mule, 168
Caffè Borghetti
  Done and Dusted, 65
Cahn, Matt, 198–199
Calabrian Chile Simple Syrup
  Gettin' Chili Out, 228–229
  recipe, 229
Caleño Light and Zesty Non-Alcoholic Spirit
  Free Bird (NA), 55
Caletta, 202–203
CALPICO concentrate
  Kasugai Sour, 237
Cappelletti
  Bitchin' Camaro, 221
Cardamaro
  The War on Christmas, 241
carrots
  Beet It, 108–109
  Beet-and-Carrot Gin Infusion, 109
  Carrot Gastrique, 125
  Carrot Me Home, 124–125
Caskey, Robert, 65
Celebrity Skin, 218
celery bitters
  Les Paul, 130–131
  Seawater Margarita, 198–199
Centerbe Faccia Brutto
  Celebrity Skin, 218
  Vietnam Bar, 188–189
Chai Tea–Infused Bourbon
  Fall Seasonal Old Fashioned, 161
  recipe, 161

Chairman's Aperitivo, The
  Negroni, 170
Chareau
  Charmed, I'm Sure, 29
Charlie Was a Sinner, 65, 66
Charmed, I'm Sure, 29
chartreuse, yellow
  The Butcher, 72
cherry liquid
  Smoke & Barrels, 193
Childs, Danny, 238–239
chocolate bitters
  Espresso Martini, 173
  Signed, Sealed, Delivered, 22
chocolate liqueur
  W Philadelphia, 51
Cicala, 210
Cicala, Joe, 210
cider
  Cider Gin Fizz, 156
  for home bar, 9
Cinnamon-Infused Rye Whiskey
  Rocket Fuel, 140
citric acid
  Lime Cordial, 79
  Neck Brace, 79
citrus, juicing, 11
City Tavern, 13–14
Classic Mojito, 113
Classic Whiskey Sour, 213
clementine juice
  The Pleasure Club of Fiumedinisi, 210
Clover Club, 15–16, 180–181
club soda
  Classic Mojito, 113
  Limoncello Fresco Spritz, 145
  Pensylvania Punch, 182
  Siam Spritz, 44
  Sip Your Sins, 66
Cocchi Americano
  Agave Vesper, 75
  Bastia Spritz, 204–205
  Bay Leaf–Infused Cocchi Americano, 205
  Siam Spritz, 44
cocoa powder
  Cocoa Blend, 65
  Done and Dusted, 65
Coconut Foam
  The Sacred Cow, 34–35
coconut liqueur
  The Sacred Cow, 34–35
coconut milk
  Bolo's Coconut Cream, 103
  Coconut Foam, 34–35
  Lollove Village, 202–203
  Passion Fruit-Coconut Syrup, 203
  Piña Colada, 103
  The Sacred Cow, 34–35
coconut water
  Apple Cordial, 110
  Coconut Foam, 34–35
  Pear of Apples, 110–111
  Piña Colobsta, 128–129
  The Sacred Cow, 34–35
Coconut-Infused Mezcal
  recipe, 195
  Tonique, 194–195

coffee extract
  Spiced Coffee Syrup, 77
coffee liqueur
  Espresso Martini, 173
  Golden Revolver, 163
  Haymaker, 56–57
  W Philadelphia, 51
coffee/espresso
  Espresso Martini, 173
  Golden Revolver, 163
  Haymaker, 56–57
  Vanilla Coffee Cream, 56–57
  W Philadelphia, 51
cognac
  Fish House Punch, 39
  Piña Colobsta, 128–129
  Signed, Sealed, Delivered, 22
  Spiced Cognac, 129
Cointreau
  Ginger Margarita, 84–85
Combier Liqueur de Rose
  Islay Roses on Your Grave, 127
Condesa and El Techo, 40, 43
Continental Midtown, The, 87
Corbishley, Ceallaigh, 186–187, 188–189
Corn Husk Syrup
  Our Daily Vedge, 225
  recipe, 225
Cosmic Sherbet
  Astronaut, 87
  recipe, 87
Craine, Jess, 188–189
cranberry juice
  Frozen Blood Orange Margarita, 88
cream liqueur
  Done and Dusted, 65
cream of coconut
  Bitchin' Camaro, 221
  Bolo's Coconut Cream, 103
  Paradise Rum Punch, 114
  Piña Colada, 103
Crémant de Bourgogne
  Raspberry Lychee Bellini, 83
crème de banane
  Neck Brace, 79
  Signed, Sealed, Delivered, 22
crème de pamplemousse rose
  Paloma, 43
  Seawater Margarita, 198–199
  Spritz Royale, 95
crème de violette
  Moonjuice, 186–187
Cross, Ian, 212, 213
Cuba Libre, 113, 114
cucumber/cucumber juice
  Cucumber Vodka, 120
  Green Juice, 225
  Green Light, 207
  Kimono Racer, 73
  Lucky Number, 133
  Mezcal Margarita, 40
  Midsummer Night, 120
  Our Daily Vedge, 225
  Pimm's Deluxe, 100
  Szechuan Pickles, 73
curaçao yuzu
  Highway Robbery, 242

250 — INDEX

Dandelion, The, 100
Darrow, Kyle, 174, 189, 193
Day, Alex, 17
Deacon, Charles, 15
Deacon, Mary R., 15–16
Dear Daphni, 62–63
Dear Daphni House Grenadine
  Persian Paloma, 62–63
  recipe, 63
Demerara Simple Syrup
  Awaji-Musubi, 69
  Free Bird (NA), 55
  Lawless Doings, 26–27
  recipe, 11
Deranged Lumberjack Old Fashioned, 52
Devern, Christopher, 116–117
Dias, Nico, 24, 26–27, 29
Dill Tincture
  Best Served Cold 2.0, 36–37
  recipe, 36
Dirty Pasta Water Martini, 174
Dolin Génépy le Chamois Liqueur
  Celebrity Skin, 218
  Islay Roses on Your Grave, 127
  Margarita Vert, 60–61
Done and Dusted, 65
Double Knot, 69
double straining, 10
dry shake, 10
eau de vie
  Untitled, 244
egg whites
  Awaji-Musubi, 69
  Bartender for Hire, 116–117
  Classic Whiskey Sour, 213
  Clover Club, 180–181
  French Breakfast, 58–59
  Gettin' Chili Out, 228–229
  Lucky Number, 133
  The Pleasure Club of Fiumedinisi, 210
  Sadōtini, 238–239
El Vez, 88, 91
elderflower cordial
  Raspberry Lychee Base, 83
  Raspberry Lychee Bellini, 83
elderflower liqueur
  Fish House Punch, 39
  Limoncello Fresco Spritz, 145
  Peach Brandy, 39
Enswell, 56–57
Espresso Martini, 173
espresso/coffee
  Espresso Martini, 173
  Golden Revolver, 163
  Haymaker, 56–57
  Vanilla Coffee Cream, 56–57
  W Philadelphia, 51
Falernum
  Paradise Rum Punch, 114
falernum liqueur
  The Butcher, 72
Fall Seasonal Old Fashioned, 161
Fat-Washed Rum Blend
  Piña Colobsta, 128–129
  recipe, 129
Felipe Collins, 91
Fell to Earth Vermouth, 244

Fernet-Branca
  No Call, No Show, 185
  Strawberry Street, 136–137
Fiorella, 174
Fiori di Sicilia, 160
Fish House Punch, 12, 39
Fork, 140, 141
Forsythia, 122–123, 124–125, 127, 128–129
48 Record Bar, 130–131, 133
Franklin Mortgage and Investment Company, 17, 30–31, 32–33, 36–37
Free Bird (NA), 55
French Breakfast, 58–59
French Breakfast Tea Simple Syrup, 59
Friday Saturday Sunday, 240, 241
Frozen Blood Orange Margarita, 88
Fusco, Jacob, 79
Garbinski, Bonnie, 169
Garden Smash, 118
gentian apéritif
  Fiori di Sicilia, 160
Gettin' Chili Out, 228–229
Ghost Pepper Tincture
  recipe, 189
  Vietnam Bar, 188–189
Giffard Banane du Brésil
  Agave Vesper, 75
  Bitchin' Camaro, 221
  Sip Your Sins, 66
  Tamale Old Fashioned, 169
gin
  Beet It, 108–109
  Beet-and-Carrot Gin Infusion, 109
  Best Served Cold 2.0, 36–37
  Cider Gin Fizz, 156
  Clover Club, 180–181
  French Breakfast, 58–59
  Good, Giving & Game, 166–167
  for home bar, 9
  Jasmine Tea–Infused Gin, 44
  Kimono Racer, 73
  Ladies Like Gin & Tonic, 164
  Lawless Doings, 26–27
  Les Paul, 130–131
  Lox-Infused Gin, 36
  Mango-Infused Gin, 27
  Moonjuice, 186–187
  Negroni, 170
  No Call, No Show, 185
  Pensylvania Punch, 182
  Pimm's Deluxe, 100
  The Pleasure Club of Fiumedinisi, 210
  Prickly Pear Wasabi Mule, 168
  Sadōtini, 238–239
  Saffron-Infused Gin, 167
  Siam Spritz, 44
  Untitled, 244
ginger
  Piña Colobsta, 128–129
  Spiced Cognac, 129
ginger beer
  Prickly Pear Wasabi Mule, 168
  Sip Your Sins, 66
ginger bitters
  Carrot Me Home, 124–125

Ginger Juice
  Ginger Syrup, 77
  recipe, 49
  Sacrifice to the Gods, 76–77
  10th Street Stretch, 48–49
Ginger Lime Syrup
  Ginger Margarita, 84–85
  recipe, 85
ginger liqueur
  Beet It, 108–109
Ginger Margarita, 84–85
Ginger Salt
  Ginger Margarita, 84–85
  recipe, 85
Ginger Syrup
  recipe, 77
  The Sacred Cow, 34–35
  Sacrifice to the Gods, 76–77
Golden Beet Syrup
  recipe, 215
  Soul Fashioned, 214–215
Golden Revolver, 163
Good, Giving & Game, 166–167
Grace & Proper, 166–167
Grand Marnier Cordon Rouge
  Investment Manhattan, 99
Granny Smith Apple Cordial
  recipe, 33
  Waiting for the Moon to Rise, 32–33
grapefruit bitters
  Persian Paloma, 62–63
grapefruit juice
  Islay Roses on Your Grave, 127
  Paloma, 43
  Seadog, 46
  Seawater Margarita, 198–199
  Spritz Royale, 95
grapefruit liqueur
  Rocket Fuel, 140
grapefruit peel
  Good, Giving & Game, 166–167
grapefruit soda
  Paloma, 43
  Persian Paloma, 62–63
  Seadog, 46
grappa
  Fiori di Sicilia, 160
Green Juice
  Our Daily Vedge, 225
  recipe, 225
Green Light, 207
Greenleaf, Randall, 151
Gregory, Derek, 216
grenadine
  Dear Daphni House Grenadine, 63
  Persian Paloma, 62–63
Grubb, John, 193
Guava Paste Syrup
  It's All Guava, Baby, 222–223
  recipe, 223
habanero shrub bitters
  Celebrity Skin, 218
Haggerty, Michael, 242
Hale & True Cider Co., 156
Harp and Crown, 55
Harrop, Christopher, 108–109, 110–111
Haymaker, 56–57

heavy whipping cream
  Haymaker, 56–57
  Vanilla Coffee Cream, 57
Heering Cherry Liqueur
  Investment Manhattan, 99
Highway Robbery, 242
Hires, Charles, 116–117
honey
  Beet It, 108–109
  Charmed, I'm Sure, 29
  Felipe Collins, 91
  Honey Rose Syrup, 96
  Honey-Tarragon Syrup, 109
  Old Fashioned, 96
honey ginger syrup
  Fall Seasonal Old Fashioned, 161
Honey Rose Syrup
  Old Fashioned, 96
  recipe, 96
Honey Syrup
  The Boog, 139
  Good, Giving & Game, 166–167
  Mutter's Charm, 184
  Pensylvania Punch, 182
  recipe, 11, 167
Honey-Tarragon Syrup
  Beet It, 108–109
  recipe, 109
Hubsher, Matt, 136–137
In the Body of Swan, 151
International Bar, The, 186–187, 188–189
Investment Manhattan, 99
Irwin's, 158–159, 160
Islay Roses on Your Grave, 127
Italian Market Espresso Martini, 51
It's All Guava, Baby, 222–223
Izzy's Cocktail Bar, 242
Jaffa Bar, 185
Jamison, Harry, 76–77
Jasmine Tea–Infused Gin
  recipe, 44
  Siam Spritz, 44
juicing citrus, 11
juniper berries
  Spiced Coffee Syrup, 77
Kaplan, David, 17
Kasugai Sour, 237
Kimono Racer, 73
Kirk, Benjamin, 202–203, 204–205
koji
  Amazake, 239
  Sadōtini, 238–239
Kombu Broth
  recipe, 199
  Seawater Margarita, 198–199
Kumquat Superjuice
  Bay Side Snap, 232–233
  recipe, 233
La Chinesca, 216
Ladies Love Gin & Tonic, 164
Langarica, Damián, 158–159
Laughlin, Neil, 134
lavender bitters
  Highway Robbery, 242
Lavender Salt
  Margarita Vert, 60–61
  recipe, 61

Lavender Syrup
  Ladies Love Gin & Tonic, 164
  recipe, 164
Lawless Doings, 26–27
lemon bitters
  Bastia Spritz, 204–205
lemon juice
  Apple Brandy Sidecar, 171
  Astronaut, 87
  Awaji-Musubi, 69
  Bartender for Hire, 116–117
  Beet It, 108–109
  Carrot Me Home, 124–125
  Cider Gin Fizz, 156
  Classic Whiskey Sour, 213
  Clover Club, 180–181
  Felipe Collins, 91
  Fish House Punch, 39
  French Breakfast, 58–59
  Islay Roses on Your Grave, 127
  Kimono Racer, 73
  Ladies Love Gin & Tonic, 164
  Lemonana, 142
  Lucky Number, 133
  Moonjuice, 186–187
  Mutter's Charm, 184
  Our Daily Vedge, 225
  Pear of Apples, 110–111
  Pensylvania Punch, 182
  Pimm's Deluxe, 100
  Prickly Pear Wasabi Mule, 168
  The Sacred Cow, 34–35
  Siam Spritz, 44
  Signed, Sealed, Delivered, 22
  Soulmonger, 208
  Spritz Royale, 95
  Strawberry Street, 136–137
  Waiting for the Moon to Rise, 32–33
lemon peel
  The Butcher, 72
  Coconut Foam, 34–35
  The Sacred Cow, 34–35
Lemonana, 142
lemons
  The Boog, 139
  Preserved Lemon Juice, 159
  Solera Legacy, 159
Lemon-Verbena-Mint Oleo Saccharum
  Lemonana, 142
Les Paul, 130–131
Levin, Lauren, 130–131
Licor 43
  Midsummer Night, 120
  Paradise Rum Punch, 114
Lime Cordial
  Neck Brace, 79
  recipe, 79, 140
  Rocket Fuel, 140
lime juice
  Bitchin' Camaro, 221
  Blood, Sweat, and Cheers, 226
  Celebrity Skin, 218
  Classic Mojito, 113
  Free Bird (NA), 55
  Frozen Blood Orange Margarita, 88
  Garden Smash, 118
  Gettin' Chili Out, 228–229

Ginger Lime Syrup, 85
Ginger Margarita, 84–85
Good, Giving & Game, 166–167
Green Light, 207
It's All Guava, Baby, 222–223
Kasugai Sour, 237
Lime Cordial, 79
Lollove Village, 202–203
Margarita Vert, 60–61
Mezcal Margarita, 40
Midsummer Night, 120
Neck Brace, 79
Paloma, 43
Paradise Rum Punch, 114
Persian Paloma, 62–63
Piña Colobsta, 128–129
Raspberry Lychee Base, 83
Raspberry Lychee Bellini, 83
Sacrifice to the Gods, 76–77
Seawater Margarita, 198–199
Sip Your Sins, 66
Vietnam Bar, 188–189
Limoncello Fresco Spritz, 144
Little Walter's, 201
LMNO, 222–223, 225
Loch Bar, 22
Lollove Village, 202–203
Lox-Infused Gin
  Best Served Cold 2.0, 36–37
  recipe, 36
Lucky Number, 133
Luxardo Bitter Bianco
  Fiori di Sicilia, 160
lychee puree
  Raspberry Lychee Base, 83
  Raspberry Lychee Bellini, 83
MacDonald, Paul, 240, 241
madeira
  Highway Robbery, 242
  The War on Christmas, 241
Manatawny Still Works, 170, 171, 173
Mango-Infused Gin
  Lawless Doings, 26–27
  recipe, 27
maple syrup
  Deranged Lumberjack Old Fashioned, 52
  Red Wine & Burnt Sugar Agrodolce, 235
Margarita Vert, 60–61
MARSEILLE Amaro
  Carrot Me Home, 124–125
Masala Chai Syrup
  Bombay Moon, 80–81
  recipe, 81
matcha
  Sadōtini, 238–239
McCaulley, Michael, 58–59, 60–61, 62–63
McKenzie, Kerry, 156
measurement conversions, 246
Melcher, Sterling, 151
Merchant's Coffee House, 13
mezcal
  Agave Vesper, 75
  Celebrity Skin, 218
  Charmed, I'm Sure, 29
  Coconut-Infused Mezcal, 195

252 — INDEX

Margarita Vert, 60–61
Mezcal Margarita, 40
Our Daily Vedge, 225
Pear of Apples, 110–111
Smoke & Barrels, 193
Soul Fashioned, 214–215
Tamale Old Fashioned, 169
10th Street Stretch, 48–49
Tonique, 194–195
Vietnam Bar, 188–189
See also tequila
Middle Child Clubhouse, 196–197, 198–199
Midori
　Kasugai Sour, 237
　Lucky Number, 133
Midsummer Night, 120
milk
　Piña Colobsta, 128–129
Miller, Shawn, 122–123, 124–125, 127, 128–129
mineral water
　Bastia Spritz, 204–205
mint
　Classic Mojito, 113
　Green Light, 207
　Lawless Doings, 26–27
　Lemonana, 142
　Lemon-Verbena-Mint Oleo Saccharum, 142
mint bitters
　Lucky Number, 133
Mint Simple Syrup
　recipe, 189
　Vietnam Bar, 188–189
mole bitters
　Tamale Old Fashioned, 169
Monkey Shoulder
　Waiting for the Moon to Rise, 32–33
Moonjuice, 186–187
Moore, Jillian, 74, 75
Morris, The, 108–109, 110–111
Morris, Zach, 244
MSG
　Les Paul, 130–131
　MSG Solution, 216
　Ridin' Dirty, 216
Murray, Rodney, 141
Mutter's Charm, 184
My Loup, 74, 75
Neck Brace, 79
Negroni, 170
Nelms, Matt, 140, 141
Next of Kin, 189, 193, 194–195
Nichols, Andrew, 22
No Call, No Show, 185
nonalcoholic cocktails
　Free Bird (NA), 55
nopales paddles
　Green Juice, 225
　Our Daily Vedge, 225
nutmeg liqueur
　Deranged Lumberjack Old Fashioned, 52
O'Connor, Meghan, 168
Old Fashioned, 96
oleo saccharum
　Espresso Martini, 173

olive brine
　Bastia Spritz, 204–205
　Dirty Pasta Water Martini, 174
　Ridin' Dirty, 216
1 Tippling Place, 80–81
onions
　Best Served Cold 2.0, 36–37
　Red Onion Brine, 131
　Red Pickled Onion Caviar, 37
orange bitters
　The Butcher, 72
　Carrot Me Home, 124–125
　Deranged Lumberjack Old Fashioned, 52
　Fall Seasonal Old Fashioned, 161
　Old Fashioned, 96
orange blossom water
　Dear Daphni House Grenadine, 63
　Persian Paloma, 62–63
orange juice
　Astronaut, 87
　Carrot Gastrique, 125
　Cosmic Sherbet, 87
　Frozen Blood Orange Margarita, 88
　Paradise Rum Punch, 114
　Pensylvania Punch, 182
　The Pleasure Club of Fiumedinisi, 210
orange liqueur
　Apple Brandy Sidecar, 171
　Blood, Sweat, and Cheers, 226
　Mezcal Margarita, 40
　Sip Your Sins, 66
　The War on Christmas, 241
orange marmalade
　French Breakfast, 58–59
orange peel/zest
　Apple Brandy Sidecar, 171
　Untitled, 244
orgeat
　Haymaker, 56–57
　The Sacred Cow, 34–35
　Our Daily Vedge, 225
Paloma, 43
Panorama Wine Bar, 144
Paradise Rum Punch, 114
Parc, 95
Parsley Oil
　Les Paul, 130–131
　recipe, 131
passion fruit liqueur
　Lollove Village, 202–203
Passion Fruit-Coconut Syrup
　Lollove Village, 202–203
　recipe, 203
Pasta Water Martini, Dirty, 174
Peach Brandy
　Fish House Punch, 39
　recipe, 39
Pear Cider, Poached, 111
Pear of Apples, 110–111
Pearl and Mary Oyster Bar, 46
Pensylvania Punch, 182
peppercorns, black
　Masala Chai Syrup, 81
　Red Pickled Onion Caviar, 37
　Spiced Coffee Syrup, 77
peppercorns, Szechuan

Balsamic Syrup, 73
Kimono Racer, 73
Szechuan Pickles, 73
peppers
　Ghost Pepper Tincture, 189
　Green Juice, 225
　Our Daily Vedge, 225
　Vietnam Bar, 188–189
Persian Paloma, 62–63
Petraske, Sasha, 17
Peychaud's bitters
　APP Bitters, 29
　The Butcher, 72
　Charmed, I'm Sure, 29
　Soulmonger, 208
　Tonique, 194–195
Philadelphia Distilling, 180–181, 182, 184
pickle juice
　Pilkarz, 201
Pilkarz, 201
pimento aromatic bitters
　APP Bitters, 29
　Charmed, I'm Sure, 29
pimento peppers
　Red Pimento & Radish Juice, 49
　10th Street Stretch, 48–49
Pimm's Deluxe, 100
Piña Colada, 103
Piña Colobsta, 128–129
pineapple juice
　Bitchin' Camaro, 221
　Celebrity Skin, 218
　Free Bird (NA), 55
　Gettin' Chili Out, 228–229
　Lollove Village, 202–203
　Paradise Rum Punch, 114
　Piña Colada, 103
　Piña Colobsta, 128–129
　Sip Your Sins, 66
pineapple liqueur
　Waiting for the Moon to Rise, 32–33
Pleasure Club of Fiumedinisi, The, 210
plum wine
　Awaji-Musubi, 69
Poached Pear Cider
　Pear of Apples, 110–111
　recipe, 111
Poison Heart, 218, 221
pomegranate juice
　Blood, Sweat, and Cheers, 226
　Dear Daphni House Grenadine, 63
　Persian Paloma, 62–63
Post Haste, 230, 232–233, 234–235
Preserved Lemon Juice
　recipe, 159
　Solera Legacy, 158–159
Pressman, Stephen, 40, 43
Prickly Pear Wasabi Mule, 168
prosecco
　Bastia Spritz, 204–205
　Kimono Racer, 73
　Limoncello Fresco Spritz, 145
　Lollove Village, 202–203
　Waiting for the Moon to Rise, 32–33
Pub on Passyunk East, The, 161

INDEX — 253

radishes
  Red Pimento & Radish Juice, 49
  10th Street Stretch, 48–49
Ranstead Room, 17, 24, 26–27, 29
raspberries
  Clover Club, 180–181
  Raspberry Lychee Base, 83
  Raspberry Lychee Bellini, 83
  Raspberry Syrup, 181
Rayer, Ryan, 166–167
Red Miso
  recipe, 48
  10th Street Stretch, 48–49
Red Onion Brine
  Les Paul, 130–131
  recipe, 131
Red Owl Tavern, 116–117, 118
Red Pickled Onion Caviar
  Best Served Cold 2.0, 36–37
  recipe, 37
Red Pimento & Radish Juice
  recipe, 49
  10th Street Stretch, 48–49
Red Wine & Burnt Sugar Agrodolce
  That's Fashion Baby! 234–235
Red Wine Foam, 233
Rhubarb Syrup
  recipe, 137
  Strawberry Street, 136–137
rice
  Amazake, 239
  Sadōtini, 238–239
Rich Demerara Simple Syrup
  recipe, 11
  Sacrifice to the Gods, 76–77
Rich Simple Syrup
  Sadōtini, 238–239
Ridin' Dirty, 216
Rittenhouse Square Straight Rye Whiskey, 13
Roberts, Devan, 193
Rocket Fuel, 140
Root Beer Reduction
  Bartender for Hire, 116–117
  recipe, 117
rosemary
  The Boog, 139
  Rosemary Simple Syrup, 46
  Seadog, 46
rosewater
  Honey Rose Syrup, 96
  Old Fashioned, 96
rum
  Bitchin' Camaro, 221
  Cacao Nibs–Infused Rum, 35
  Charmed, I'm Sure, 29
  Classic Mojito, 113
  Fat-Washed Rum Blend, 129
  Fish House Punch, 39
  Lollove Village, 202–203
  Neck Brace, 79
  Paradise Rum Punch, 114
  Piña Colada, 103
  Piña Colobsta, 128–129
  Rocket Fuel, 140
  The Sacred Cow, 34–35
  Sacrifice to the Gods, 76–77
  Signed, Sealed, Delivered, 22
  Sip Your Sins, 66
  White Chocolate Rum, 203

rye whiskey
  Bay Side Snap, 232–233
  BP Manhattan, 92
  Cinnamon-Infused Rye Whiskey, 140
  Investment Manhattan, 99
  Old Fashioned, 96
  Rocket Fuel, 140
  Smoke & Barrels, 193
  Soulmonger, 208
  That's Fashion Baby! 234–235
Sacred Cow, The, 34–35
Sacrifice to the Gods, 76–77
Sadōtini, 238–239
Saffron-Infused Gin
  Good, Giving & Game, 166–167
  recipe, 167
Salers Gentian Apéritif
  Fiori di Sicilia, 160
  Neck Brace, 79
Saline Solution
  Espresso Martini, 173
  Moonjuice, 186–187
  recipe, 11, 187
  Rocket Fuel, 140
  Scorched Atlas, 141
  Seadog, 46
salmon
  Best Served Cold 2.0, 36–37
  Lox-Infused Gin, 36
salting a rim, 11
Sampan, 44
Sassafras, 134, 136–137
Schulson, Michael, 58–59
Scorched Atlas, 141
Scotch whiskey
  Islay Roses on Your Grave, 127
  Scorched Atlas, 141
  Waiting for the Moon to Rise, 32–33
Scott, Rob, 237
Scrappy's Fire Tincture
  Margarita Vert, 60–61
Seadog, 46
Seawater Margarita, 198–199
Serpentine, Chris, 69
shaking, 10
shaoxing wine
  Ridin' Dirty, 216
Shayer, Canyon, 184
sherry, dry
  Investment Manhattan, 99
sherry, fino
  Scorched Atlas, 141
  Seadog, 46
sherry, oloroso
  Signed, Sealed, Delivered, 22
  Solera Legacy, 158–159
sherry, Pedro Ximénez
  Solera Legacy, 158–159
shochu
  Kasugai Sour, 237
  Sadōtini, 238–239
Siam Spritz, 44
Signed, Sealed, Delivered, 22
Simple Syrup
  Agave Simple Syrup, 61
  Apple Brandy Sidecar, 171
  Calabrian Chile Simple Syrup, 229
  Cider Gin Fizz, 156

Classic Whiskey Sour, 213
Coconut Foam, 34–35
Demerara Simple Syrup, 11
Fish House Punch, 39
French Breakfast Tea Simple Syrup, 59
Frozen Blood Orange Margarita, 88
Gettin' Chili Out, 228–229
Golden Revolver, 163
Green Light, 207
Mint Simple Syrup, 189
Peach Brandy, 39
Pimm's Deluxe, 100
Piña Colobsta, 128–129
recipe, 11
Rich Demerara Simple Syrup, 11
Rosemary Simple Syrup, 46
The Sacred Cow, 34–35
Sadōtini, 238–239
Seawater Margarita, 198–199
Siam Spritz, 44
10th Street Stretch, 48–49
Tonique, 194–195
Vanilla Bean Simple Syrup, 187
Sip Your Sins, 66
SkyHigh Lounge, 83, 84–85
Smoke & Barrels, 193
soda water
  Green Light, 207
  Lawless Doings, 26–27
Solera Legacy, 158–159
Soul Fashioned, 214–215
Soulmonger, 208
South Philadelphia Tap Room, 163, 164
Southwark, 151
sparkling water
  Spritz Royale, 95
spearmint
  Classic Mojito, 113
Special, The, 155
Spiced Coffee Syrup
  recipe, 77
  Sacrifice to the Gods, 76–77
Spiced Cognac
  Piña Colobsta, 128–129
  recipe, 129
Spiced Demerara Syrup
  recipe, 159
  Solera Legacy, 158–159
Spritz Royale, 95
St. Oner's, 207, 208
Starr, Stephen, 17
Stateside Vodka Distillery, 226, 228–229
Stipo, Vince, 56–57
stirring, 10
straining, 10
Stratus Rooftop Lounge, 120
strawberries
  Garden Smash, 118
  It's All Guava, Baby, 222–223
  Midsummer Night, 120
  Strawberry Infused Tequila-and-Aperol Blend, 118
  Strawberry Puree, 136
  Strawberry Salt, 222
  Strawberry Street, 136–137
  Strawberry Syrup, 120

sugarcane juice
　Classic Mojito, 113
　Paradise Rum Punch, 114
　Szechuan Pickles
　　Kimono Racer, 73
　　recipe, 73
Tamale Old Fashioned, 169
Tang
　Astronaut, 87
　Cosmic Sherbet, 87
Tasmania Bitters Mountain Pepperberry
　Soul Fashioned, 214–215
tea, black
　French Breakfast, 58–59
　French Breakfast Tea Simple Syrup, 59
tea, chai
　Bombay Moon, 81
　Chai Tea–Infused Bourbon, 161
　Fall Seasonal Old Fashioned, 161
　Masala Chai Syrup, 81
　The Sacred Cow, 34–35
tea, jasmine
　Jasmine Tea–Infused Gin, 44
　Siam Spritz, 44
tea, rishi peach
　Fish House Punch, 39
　Peach Brandy, 39
techniques, 10–11
10th Street Stretch, 48–49
tequila
　Agave Vesper, 75
　Done and Dusted, 65
　Felipe Collins, 91
　Frozen Blood Orange Margarita, 88
　Garden Smash, 118
　Ginger Margarita, 84–85
　Green Light, 207
　It's All Guava, Baby, 222–223
　Margarita Vert, 60–61
　Paloma, 43
　Persian Paloma, 62–63
　Seawater Margarita, 198–199
　Strawberry Infused Tequila-and-Aperol Blend, 118
　See also mezcal
That's Fashion Baby! 234–235
Thrash, Brandon, 196–197, 198–199
tiki bitters
　Neck Brace, 79
Toasted Almond-Infused Bianco Vermouth
　Fiori di Sicilia, 160
Tobacco-Infused White Vermouth
　BP Manhattan, 92
　recipe, 92
tomatillos
　Green Juice, 225
　Our Daily Vedge, 225
tonic water
　Ladies Love Gin & Tonic, 164
　Sacrifice to the Gods, 76–77
Tonique, 194–195
Trestle Inn, The, 212, 213, 214–215
triple sec
　Astronaut, 87

Frozen Blood Orange Margarita, 88
Green Light, 207
Twisted Tail, The, 139
Ulsh, Andrea, 221
Untitled, 244
Vanilla Bean Simple Syrup
　Moonjuice, 186–187
　recipe, 187
Vanilla Coffee Cream
　Haymaker, 56–57
　recipe, 57
Vanilla-Infused Vodka
　Gettin' Chili Out, 228–229
　recipe, 228–229
Vanille de Madagascar
　Bartender for Hire, 116–117
　Lollove Village, 202–203
velvet falernum
　Celebrity Skin, 218
verbena
　Lemonana, 142
　Lemon-Verbena-Mint Oleo Saccharum, 142
vermouth
　for home bar, 9
vermouth, bianco
　Best Served Cold 2.0, 36–37
　Fiori di Sicilia, 160
　Toasted Almond-Infused Bianco Vermouth, 160
vermouth, dry
　Clover Club, 180–181
　Les Paul, 130–131
　The Pleasure Club of Fiumedinisi, 210
　Raspberry Syrup, 181
　Untitled, 244
vermouth, sweet
　Les Paul, 130–131
　Negroni, 170
　No Call, No Show, 185
　Red Wine & Burnt Sugar Agrodolce, 235
　Scorched Atlas, 141
vermouth, white
　BP Manhattan, 92
　Tobacco-Infused White Vermouth, 92
Vernick Fish, 39
Vetri, Marc, 174
Vietnam Bar, 188–189
Vigo Amaro
　W Philadelphia, 51
vinegar, red wine
　Red Wine & Burnt Sugar Agrodolce, 235
vodka
　Best Served Cold 2.0, 36–37
　Blood, Sweat, and Cheers, 226
　Blood Orange–Infused Vodka, 226
　Cucumber Vodka, 120
　Dill Tincture, 36
　Dirty Pasta Water Martini, 174
　Gettin' Chili Out, 228–229
　for home bar, 9
　Midsummer Night, 120
　Pilkarz, 201

Ridin' Dirty, 216
Sadōtini, 238–239
Vanilla-Infused Vodka, 228–229
W Philadelphia, 51
vodka, citrus
　Lucky Number, 133
vodka, peach
　Astronaut, 87
W Philadelphia, 48–49, 51
Waiting for the Moon to Rise, 32–33
Walsh, Kevin, 161
War on Christmas, The, 241
Wasabi Syrup
　Prickly Pear Wasabi Mule, 168
　recipe, 168
Washington, George, 12, 13
Weintraub, Wei-Wei, 30–31, 32–33, 34–35
whey
　Moonjuice, 186–187
whiskey
　about, 13
　Awaji-Musubi, 69
　Espresso Martini, 173
　Haymaker, 56–57
　Highway Robbery, 242
　for home bar, 9
　Soul Fashioned, 214–215
　See also bourbon; rye whiskey; Scotch whiskey
White Chocolate Rum
　Lollove Village, 202–203
　recipe, 203
Wilder, 70–71, 72, 73
Wilfred's Non-Alcoholic Aperitif
　Free Bird (NA), 55
Williams, Gregg "The Boog," 139
wine, plum
　Awaji-Musubi, 69
wine, red
　Red Wine & Burnt Sugar Agrodolce, 235
　Red Wine Foam, 233
　That's Fashion Baby! 234–235
wine, shaoxing
　Ridin' Dirty, 216
wine, sparkling
　Bastia Spritz, 204–205
　Kimono Racer, 73
　Limoncello Fresco Spritz, 145
　Lollove Village, 202–203
　Waiting for the Moon to Rise, 32–33
Xolalpa, Isai, 48–49
yogurt
　Coconut Foam, 34–35
　The Sacred Cow, 34–35
Young, Drew, 66
yuzu juice
　Kasugai Sour, 237
yuzu liqueur
　Kimono Racer, 73
Za'atar Salt
　Persian Paloma, 62–63
　recipe, 63
Zahav, 142
Zingler, Chris, 80–81

—About Cider Mill Press Book Publishers—

Good ideas ripen with time. From seed to harvest, Cider Mill Press brings fine reading, information, and entertainment together between the covers of its creatively crafted books. Our Cider Mill bears fruit twice a year, publishing a new crop of titles each spring and fall.

"Where Good Books Are Ready for Press"
501 Nelson Place
Nashville, Tennessee 37214
cidermillpress.com

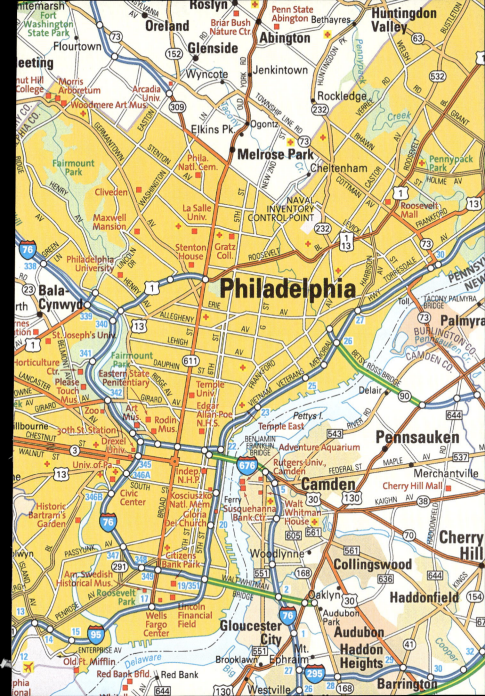

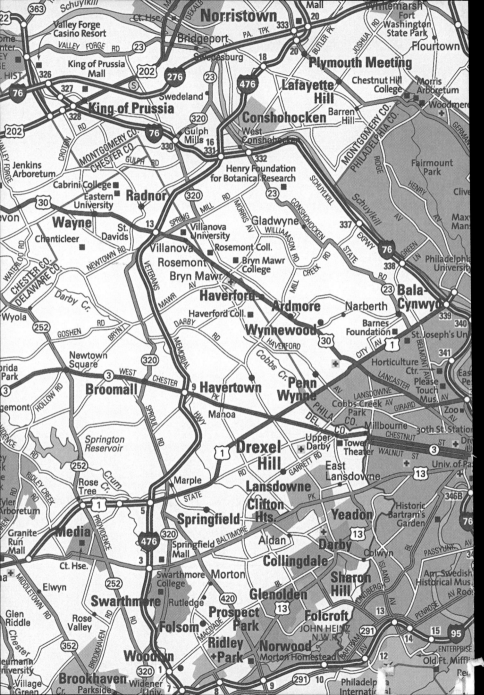